ALMOST EATEN !

By Danny McGee, trout fisherman

Face to face with wild bears from Yosemite to Pacific Northwest and lived to tell the tale

Introduction

If you are planning on venturing into bear country, let Danny McGee give you some sound advice, as you follow the author re-living his true life experiences keeping one step away from being eaten by hungry bears chasing after his most prized possession, rainbow trout!

What would *you* do, if you met a wild bear on a trail? Scream, freeze like a statue, or run, forgetting about the two legs you have and the four legs the bear has. One day the bear, or bears, will scare you out of your wits and maybe give you a good laugh while they destroy your camping gear looking for a morsel of food, before looking at you as the next meal.

Can you pass a humorous test provided by a person who has actually been face to face with more than one big bear?

After reading the following pages, you just might know what to do when confronting a wild bear!

TABLE OF CONTENTS

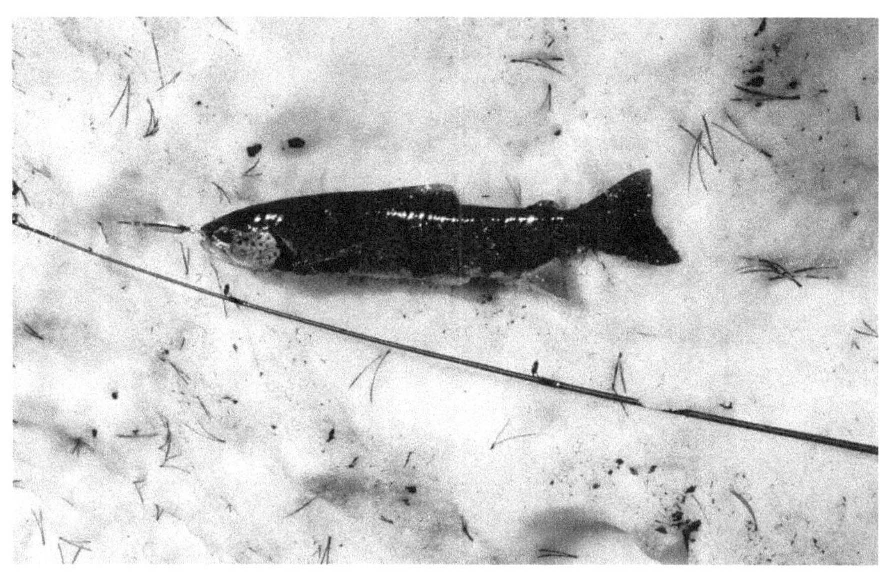

CHAPTER 1
HOOKED FOR LIFE

You are going hiking and tent camping with a few friends in bear country and stop at a local outdoor store to buy supplies.

A. Would you purchase the entire bear deterrents available, a bell to wear on your belt, a whistle, an air horn and any new gadgets they might have for sale?

B. Purchase candy bars, Oreos, potato chips, trail mix and all your favorite snacks to munch on while on the trail. After all, you are on vacation and forget "A," because you are not in grizzly country but black bear country. Black bears are vegetarians so you not part of the bear's food chain.

C. Besides, your friend bought plenty of bear deterrents and will protect you.

**The answers to the questions are located at the end of each chapter.*

All a good trout fisherman ever thinks about is catching beautiful trout fish morning, noon and night. Whether it is rainbow, golden, brook, cut throat or brown trout really makes only a small difference. What does make a big difference to a trout fisherman is of course the luck and skill that was used in catching these elusive tranquil fish. The size, how many on the end of a stringer and most important, where the trout fish were caught!

And just like trout fisherman, hungry wild bears also think about beautiful trout fish morning, noon, and night. To a hungry bear's empty stomach, I don't think it makes much difference if the trout are rainbow, golden, brook, cut throat or brown. To a wild three hundred pound bear, I am sure the size of the trout is what matters most of all and how many trout will it take to fill such a big stomach. What skill the bear uses in acquiring the fish, even if that means stealing the trout from a trout fisherman, does not matter one bit!

How does a person become a serious trout fisherman? How does one become so focused on trout fishing that the person's entire life evolves around catching a fish, a simple little trout fish?

The trout fishing bug is sometimes put in a child's head by the trout fishing dad and sometimes even a trout fishing mom, or by unsuspecting non-fishing parents who go on Sunday picnics at nearby lakes and give their kids fishing poles on warm sunny days just for something to do. Never really thinking that one of them might actually catch a fish but then with one little, "I got one, I got one!!!" The excitement runs through every vein in that little body, it's completely overwhelming, coming from deep within a human prehistoric mind of capturing food.

The adrenalin of something new and exciting latches on to a kid just like seeing a new bicycle under the Christmas tree except this time instead of a bicycle, it's a slippery flip flopping sparkling fish on the end of a line. The fishing bug has now hooked yet another innocent soul making the whole meaning of their lives forever bound to becoming a trout fisherman.

Now being a trout fisherman is not such a bad thing. On the contrary they have a very good reputation. I even once heard a story of a poor old man who wasn't a trout fisherman at all and could not even stand the smell of fish but he did enjoy taking Sunday naps lying down on the grass by the side of the lake. This he found out was not such a good idea because just about everyone who walked by would stop and ask him if he was ok having a heart attack, stroke or something. They were also curious to see if he wasn't about to steal someone's picnic basket. The fellow figured out that if he had a fishing pole next to him, a small rock tied on the end of the line in the water, everyone who pass by just left him alone saying, "It's just a trout fisherman waiting for a bite." Such is the good reputation of a trout fisherman.

For me, it was my non fishing dad who taught me about fishing. I never ever saw him with a fishing pole when I was younger, my dad loved the great out doors and took us kids on all kinds of camping trips, yep, and he loved those picnics. He would of course always bring along fishing poles for us unsuspecting kids luring us into a future life of fishing without even knowing it.

To this day, I can still remember when I was eight years old and caught my first rainbow trout. It was on the same day my brother caught the biggest one of all!

My family decided to vacation on the eastern side of the High Sierras staying in one of the cabins at Kit Carson lodge right on Silver Lake. Kit Carson Lodge was named after the great mountain man, guide, and United States explorer Kit Carson, who lived in the early eighteen hundreds a time of stage coaches, free roaming Indians, migrating buffalos and wild lawless towns.

On the first morning, my older brother William and I, Danny, woke up early, all excited to get out on the lakeshore and start fishing! Running out the cabin door with a few buns for breakfast, fishing pole and tackle box in hand, the excitement of catching a trout was only a make believe dream until now.

The crisp cool morning air gave us an extra spark under our feet to start running even faster down to the lake but, the running eventually came to a slow crawl as I followed William maneuvering over fallen pine trees, large rocks and trying not to be eaten alive by sharp scratchy needle bushes jumping out attacking us.

After walking what seemed like half way around Silver Lake, William found a spot on top of a giant granite boulder. We both looked down into the deep pool of aqua blue green water and smiled. It was perfect for fishing.

Looking out over the lake, I could see a performance of sparkling bright glitter on the surface, reminding me of rhinestone ballet dancers jumping out and around in every direction.

The windless sunny morning created a perfectly clear mirror on the water, reflecting a thick green ribbon of forest around the lake, surrounded above by towering rugged snow capped mountain peaks.

When you are in places like this, you can forget about fishing altogether, and just daydream the day away while gazing spellbound at the alpine beauty of the High Sierras. But this was fishing, and fishing meant concentrating.

There we sat, concentrating on our drooping fishing lines, staring at the bright red salmon egg on the end of the hook in the water floating up from the sandy bottom, not saying a word, waiting patiently for a little nibble.

According to my brother's watch a half hour had gone by and neither of us has had even a smither of a tug. Another half hour went by, nothing. William got up, saying he couldn't sit all day waiting for a fish to bite; he was going to snag one. Opening the tackle box, rummaging around finding what he was looking for, switching out his salmon egg to a bright silver metal spinner with a red plastic tail. In a matter of seconds he was casting far out into the lake slowly reeling the lure in.

The warm sun was now upon us, my dry throat started to remember something we had forgotten. Standing up, trying not to loose my balance and fall into the sharp needle bush below, I slowly moved behind William, "Hey, I'm thirsty. I'm going back to the cabin to get the canteen we forgot."

William tried to looked at me over one shoulder, then the other while reeling in his line, when we finally met eye to eye I could read the expression on his face, "Why are you even talking to me, can't you see I'm doing serious fishing here?"

What my brother said next made me feel quite stupid, "why don't you just drink the lake!?"

I mean, hey, he was right. Here in front of us was a beautiful clean lake created from the freshly melted snow tricking down from the High Sierra mountain range. What could be better than that? I was going to go all the way back to the cabin just for a little drink of water? Now, that didn't make any sense at all.

From than on, I always knew my older brother was smarter than me, because he had more common sense. I mean, why I didn't think of it, "Just drink the lake!"

I really admired my brother for not saying something like, "Stupid brother." Although, I'm sure that did cross his mind.

Turning around to go back to my own fishing spot, I tried to dodge another of William's cast thinking, "just drink the lake, just drink the lake," when I heard William yelling in excitement, "I got one, I got one!!!"

As he pulled the fishing pole back hard, the back of my ear pulled forward in excruciating pain. He pulled back yelling, "I got one, I got one!"

I pulled back yelling, "eeeooow, ooow!"

He pulled and I yelled, but this time he started reeling in line saying, "It's the biggest fish I ever caught!!!"

He pulled back again; I pulled back yelling, "ahhhhhhh eeeooooow!!!" He pulled and reeled, I yelled until I was right up to the top of William's fishing pole!

Gritting his teeth with the look of, "I'm going to get you for this," was all over his face. He was madder then a hornet! Why? Because I wasn't a real fish!

"What kind of an idiot brother ends up on the end of a fishing pole? If I wasn't fishing, I would… that's it; I'm not fishing with you any more! I'm going to find my own spot!"

With that said, he pulled out a small pocket knife cutting the stretched fishing line at the reel, picked up his tackle box and walked away leaving me with a bright silver fishing lure dangling at the end of my bleeding ear. He didn't even try to help me get the hook out saying it was my own stupid fault to stand behind him.

You might think I was having a bad fishing day, sitting all alone on that big rock trying to pull the hook out with some rusty old needle nose pliers with the lingering smell of old fish guts. Twisting the hook first one way, while tearing off a little more skin as the barb on the hook dug in a little deeper, then the other way dripping lots of bright red blood all over my white t-shirt, "ouch!"

With all my attention focus on the immediate surgery, I had forgotten all about my fishing pole that was now spinning the reel around at lightning speed. I dropped the pliers, grabbed the fishing pole and stopped the reel pulling the rod back hard sending a big trout out into the air of the mirror lake. The bright rainbow colored fish twisting and turned flipping water from its tail before hitting the water.

"Wow, what a fish! I had it! If only my brother could see this!"

What a fighter! The drag on the reel pulled the light rod bouncing up and down under the heavy weight. With all my might I pulled the rod up, hoping the line would not snap under the pressure, while slowly starting too real in the big fish. The rod finally gave way letting me bring the tired trout into the shallow clear water. With one big tug of the fishing pole, the great fish was out of the water and on top of the granite bolder flip flopping all over the place. Setting the pole down, I carefully picked up the squirming fish with two hands admiring the brilliant wet rainbow colors; blue, green, yellow, red, "Wow, about eighteen inches I'd say."

While studying the sleek form, inspecting every fin, I could not help to think what a magnificent perfect creature I held in my hands. Then I saw my golden hook sticking right through the upper lip of the fish's mouth dripping with dark red blood. My ear started to throb feeling the weight of the lure hanging on my earlobe and now I could feel the pain of the fish.

"Man," I said to the fish, "that hook in your mouth must hurt just as much as the lure hanging on my ear."

I really did not want to cause this fish any more pain, and I just couldn't see eating something I had such a connection with, even if the connection was pain. For some reason, I had the strange feeling the fish was talking back to me asking, "How would you like to be eaten by a giant monster with lots of sharp teeth?" Of course I had to answer back, "No, I would not like to be eaten by a big monster with sharp teeth."

Firmly holding the slippery fish with one hand on the ground, I very carefully removed the sharp hook from its bleeding lip. I pick it up, holding tight to its slimy body with both hands and slowly made my way down off the boulder bringing the squirming fish to the waters edge. Ever so gently, not wanting to injure one fin, I held the fish upright in the icy water giving it time to collect its equilibrium. The fish quickly squirmed out of my hands and swam into the deep blue water probably wondering, like I was, how long it would take for its lip to heal.

Hearing some kind of a rustling in the thick scratchy needle bushes about twenty feet to my left I looked up in excitement thinking it was my brother. What I saw made my heart beat two thousand miles a minute in instant fear! At the lake's edge stood a big bear staring right at me! The only thing that separated me from the bear was a couple of granite boulders and those bushes! Thinking to myself what a big mistake I had just made by letting the trout go, if I still had the trout, I could have thrown the fish to the bear and made a quick get away. This was not good. Will I be next on the bears menu and eaten by a monster with big sharp teeth as the trout predicted?

Slowly I lifted myself up to a standing position, ignoring the wild bear's stare saying to myself over and over, "Please don't eat me, please don't eat me. Can't you let me go, just like I let the little trout go? Please don't eat me, please don't eat me."

Carefully taking three steps back, while slowly reaching down trying not to make any fast movements, I picked up the fishing pole and tackle box in one hand. Then maneuvering in slow motion taking another step to the right, twisting my body around until I was at the edge of the boulder, I took a quick look down at the four foot drop below and saw a perfect landing spot. With one last glance I looked back at the big bear, still staring right at me, who was probably so puzzled thinking, "I can't believe what I just saw! That crazy kid just caught a perfectly good rainbow trout and threw in right back in the water! What animal would ever do such a thing?"

I jumped off the rock hitting the firm dirt, running as fast as I could jingling the sharp lure in my ear in every direction holding tight onto my fishing pole and tackle box. I ran and ran as fast as I could, not looking back once to see if that bear was right behind me and didn't stop until I burst threw the cabin door, "Mom, dad there's a bear chasing me! I caught this huge fish and the bear wanted to eat the fish and…me and…!"

My dad showed absolutely no emotion, as he sat in big cozy chair staring at me over his reading glasses. He seemed a bit annoyed a kind of, "I could care-less attitude," that I even interrupted him reading his favorite travel magazine.

"Slow down take a deep breath, you're not making any sense. You say you saw a bear? That is something, what is a fish lure doing in your ear? Did you say you caught a fish? Where is it?"

I started to explain what happen to my dad when William walked through the door with two nice ten inch rainbow trout. My dad jumped out of his chair and completely ignored what I was trying to say. "Hey, look at those fish! Rainbow trout for dinner tonight! Great job William, I guess you're the fisherman in the family!"

When William finished telling everyone how he caught the rainbow trout, I thought I would finally get a chance to tell everyone about the fish I caught and the bear who wanted to eat me. After being interrupted a zillion times by William, who said he had not seen any bear so I couldn't have seen a bear and I just made up the fish story because I was jealous, I gave up trying.

William also told our dad how I had kept running behind him while he was casting and it was my own fault for getting the fishing lure caught in my ear.

Shaking his head looking right at me with a mean tight lip expression, my Dad agreed completely with William.

Trying to change the subject after everyone thought I was a liar, making up fish and bear stories, I tried to tell my dad what a great idea William had when I got thirsty while we were fishing. I was going to go all the way back to the cabin for a canteen of water, when William told me to, "Just drink the lake!"

My dad's tight lip turned into even a meaner frown, crinkling his forehead with those squinted beady dark eyes staring right at me, "Now why would you do everything William tells you to do? Don't you know fish and who knows who what else uses the lake as a toilet? Now sit down, I'll go get some hydrogen peroxide and get that lure out! As soon as we get back home, you're going to get another tetanus shot!"

I was utterly puzzled. We can't drink the lake, but we can eat the fish out of the lake?

When I grew a little older I would find out that it is OK to drink the lake and eat the trout out of some lakes, but you can not drink or eat the fish out of other lakes because people actually use them as toilets.

After my first experience of catching a rainbow trout and hooking onto its bleeding lip, every fish I've caught from that day on, I would think back on the day when William hooked my ear and instantly feel the trout's pain. You might even think I would throw every fish I reel in back into the water to swim yet another day, and another, hoping they would die of old age. But no, after I had my very first taste of fried trout dusted with corn meal that evening at our cozy cabin by Silver Lake, I was hooked for life!

Later that same night, when our family sat drinking hot chocolate on the small porch while looking at the sun setting on Silver Lake, I heard a bear digging into the trash can over by the parking lot. He was no doubt in search of a tasty morsel of leftover trout bones, "Yep," I said to myself, "trout fishermen and bears do have a lot in common, even if the skill used to catch the trout, or scrounge for trout bones, is based on luck more than anything else. And it really doesn't matter what other people think, I know I caught that trout, and the bear knows I caught that trout!"

I also came to the realization that rainbow trout was food not only for trout fisherman but also bears who occasionally can't make up their minds whether or not to eat a trout fisherman.

Little did I realize, at that time in my young life what the unknowing, "Scare you out of your pants," future had in store for me as a trout fisherman who was now hooked for life, and the hungry bears who would be chasing after my most prize possession, rainbow trout!

ANSWERS TO CHAPTER 1 QUESTIONS

**The author does not claim to be an expert on bear behavior; just a trout fisherman trying to give some good sensible advice.*

a. Any kind of bear deterrent including air horns, pots and pans, loud whistle, is a good idea in bear country; at least it's something to defend your life with. Remember, some parks it is illegal to enter or use bear deterrent sprays of any kind including Yosemite as of this writing. Read the park rules before going, the last thing you need is a citation for just being in possession of the stuff. A whistle is a good noise maker and could help your situation by alerting other hikers to come to your defense, or the loud screeching sound is enough to scare the bear away. Some people say wearing a bell lets a bear know you are close by (dinner bell calling the bear?); scientist say the bear could have already picked up your scent long before it would hear a bell.

During one of my many camping trips, sitting around a nice glowing campfire under the stars with friends, someone asked how can you tell the difference between grizzly bear scat on the trail and black bear scat? Not wanting to give a wrong answer like grizzly poop is "huge" because it comes from a much larger bear, I answered, "I don't know, what is the difference?"

I remember being told with a grin, "Well, the grizzly scat is the one with bells in it!"

Black Bears usually don't like people and stay far away, especially if you're making a lot of noise. Bears hate noise and many bears can be scared off just by banging a couple of pots and pans together, if you're lucky.

That is, unless you have something they want, like rainbow trout cooked with bits of bacon sizzling in a pan which they have smelled you cooking from five miles away.

Now that will be a big decision you will have to make when you see three big black bears following the yummy scent running as fast as they can right for your camp.

You could run for your car, if you have one.

Or let the bears take the rainbow trout, any other food sitting around your camp site, while you calmly take pictures wondering how big a bear appetite is.

Or you could hurry up and quickly eat the trout as fast as you can dribbling bacon grease down the front of you.

Or you could grab the sizzling pan and as fast as you can, store it in a bear proof container and try to defend your campsite by yelling, waving your arms, making loud noises.

Most experts agree that if a bear has decided not to eat the trout cooked with bacon and eat you instead, than you better get ready for a fight if you want to live. Just playing dead is a last resort because the bear can still bite large chunks of meat out of you. If you run, the bear will run after you and think about it, you have two legs and the bear has four! Don't even think about climbing a tree, unless you want your feet to be eaten first!

Wave your arms, yell, throw things, look the bear in the eye letting him know you will not back down, move slowly to the side away from the bear and hopefully the bear decides you are too big of a challenge. Now would be a good time to use your air horn and loud whistle if you brought one.

If the bear will not back down, use any bear deterrent that might me available, preparation for this moment is critical! If the wind is blowing any kind of spray including cooking spray, mosquito repellent spray, sunscreen spray, deodorant spray, might not even reach the bear at all and end up in your face but it's worth a try!

Some people say spraying something into a bears face only makes the bear mad and should be used as a last resort! Turning a non-aggressive bear, who is only interested in food, into an aggressive bear that is now ready to fight his aggressor when he comes to his senses.

All bears are unpredictable; you just don't know what they will do next, including eating you!

Sometimes it's better to get a safe distance and just watch the bear or bears, devour all your food, with any luck they will be on their way. Just remember they will be back at anytime especially if you start cooking again. The bear now has a mindset that you are a food source so follow you he will, that's what makes bear proof containers so important.

The best advice is to find out as much information as possible of where the current sighting of bear activity is located and prepare diligently according to the parks rules and regulations.

b. Black bears for the most part are vegetarians but, incidences have been recorded of black bears fiercely attacking and killing people. Leaving a trail of goodies on the trail is asking for trouble and that trouble lies with a hungry bear with a never ending appetite and you!

c. Don't count on anyone protecting you, when a big wild bear enters a camp, everyone's hair on the back of their neck stands up and instantly the Stone Age adrenaline kicks into survival mode, fight or flight. In a matter of seconds you will know what kind of friends you have and what survival mode they have chosen if you're standing alone when facing a big hungry bear.

Come to think of it, I never had any of that stuff, spray's, air horn, whistle, not even a walking stick when I went backpacking in bear country and most of the time the bears did their thing and I did mine, except when I was trout fishing!

CHAPTER
2
Whoever said bad luck never follows?

What would *you* do?

You are the last person in a line of four backpackers hiking up a steep wilderness mountain trail. The lead backpacker yells to you that a big wild bear has just jumped out on the trail right behind you.

A. Stop hiking, move slowly to the side of the trail, thinking the black bear will walk right passed you because he is only interested in his berry patch further up the trail.

B. Drop your backpack let the bear tear into it and run as fast as you can up the trail, thinking the bear is only after the food you have been carrying for the last four days. Your buddies will surly share their food because they were smart enough to use bear proof food storage containers.

C. All of the backpackers forged a plan before the hike, agreeing to confront any bear if challenged for their food, and the backpacker who refused to use a bear poof container was not allowed to go on the trip.

As the years went by, I completely lost count of how many times I put on a backpack, grabbed my fishing pole and hiked, huffing and puffing mile after mile, day after day, straight up, straight down, switch back after switch back, in search of the evasive trout fish. Or, the miles I have driven trying to interpret strange looking trout fishing maps looking for that perfect spot overflowing with fish.

The winter snow on the California High Sierras mountain range was going to be melting fast; spring would be here soon, I was getting very restless to get off my behind and go do something. I was long over due, even to the point of being a bit grouchy from what my wife and daughter said. A change of scenery and some fishing is just what I needed.

It was at the end of April and I was counting on my camper shell that sat on the back of my pickup truck to keep me warm and protected from natures harsh elements. My only traveling companions would be happy thoughts of lakes and rivers jumping with big rainbow trout.

On the first day of my fishing trip, I left Sonoma County California at 3am, anxious to fish the clean mountain streams in Mt. Lassen National Park by late afternoon.

The drive didn't seem that long, traffic was good not too many cars on the road and the off ramps leading to small towns just wiz's by and in no time at all I was fishing a small crystal clear lake with red devil lures. Within the first half hour I caught four small rainbow trout about eight inches long and did the right thing releasing them all back into the lake to grow bigger.

Eventually giving up catching any big ones I took a long hike and later found a nice camp site at Manzanita Lake. At first light on my second day I was up early fishing from the lake shore, using a barb-less hook with red earth worms. I caught a nice three pound brown trout but was disappointed I could not keep it, because the lake is catch and release only.

With my trout stomach growling on such a nice sunny spring day, I drove north out of Mt. Lassen National Park, and over to Hat Creek area. The creek itself winds in and out next to the road and has a history of fisherman catching trophy size fish. Finding a turnout, I parked the truck on the side of the road and set out on foot with fishing pole in hand.

Finding the perfect spot where the fast moving white water made rippling sounds rushing over mossy rocks flowing into small deep pools of water, I reached into my fishing vest pulling out a tiny fishing box. I knew the exact dry fly to use, a reddish black winged with a white front tip and yellow tail.

On my third cast I let the white water take the fly down stream and as I pulled back the line a big trout jump out of the creek catching the fly! The fish took off swimming as fast as it could back and forth in the water as it pulled back hard against my twitching pole. I was too hungry to let this big fish get away. I pulled back on the pole again and again, eventually wearing the trout down. I reeled the fish to the edge and scooped it into my net, a nice sixteen inch brook trout!

For the rest of the day I fished up and down the creek, finally catching my limit and now as the day was coming to an end. I couldn't wait to find a camp spot to start cooking!

Hat Creek campground was right down the road, thank goodness, the black darkness of night would soon be upon me.

The evening campground was just about empty, with many good spots to choose from among the tall pine trees and small patches of snow. I found a good site, using my lantern I could see not to many cigarette butts were left on the ground and I was also impressed that most of the past campers had actually used a bucket to catch the dish water in or I might have walk into a large mud puddle and drown.

Walking back from the entrance booth after depositing the camp fee, I now faced one of the hardest decision for a trout fisherman, how to cook the daily catch of trout. I could de-bone it, spreading it out wide and tie it to a forked stick smoking it next to the camp fire, or I could barbecue it on the camp fire grill, or I could wrap it in tin foil with butter, lemon, dill and rosemary letting it sizzle on the grill, or I could pan fry it in corn meal, or pan fry it with sauté veggies with almonds, or….

Still thinking of all the delicious dinner choices, I crumble up bits of paper sticking them under the fire wood kindling I had piled up to form a tee-pee in the campfire ring. Pulling a small match book from my pocket I leaned over striking the match slowly moving the lighted flame toward the paper, igniting not the paper but some form of odorless gas that created a loud explosion of a red hot flaming fire ball in the fire pit, "Ka – Blam!!!" The force blew me completely off my feet sending me into the air before landing hard on the ground some six feet away! Stupefied, I watched a huge bright nuclear mushroom fire ball shoot straight up catching every tree limb in its path on fire as it disappeared past the tree tops right up into the dark sky. The fire ring was completely engulfed in flames as the towering inferno spew out burning red hot fire ball after fire ball into the black sky.

In one very long minute the fire ball was gone, "poof!" just like someone would blow out a candle. Thick black smoke choked the air, burnt embers from singed tree limbs popped and cracked. I was fried. My eyebrows, my eye lids and most of my hair were gone. My clothes cooked to a brown crisp and my face felt like a red hot charcoal brisket!

As I sat there trying to comprehend what just happened, people from the other campsites came running towards me asking if I was alright. Unable to speak, still in shock, someone sat me up and offered water but my trembling hand was unable to grasp the bottle, I shook my head no. My whole body was shaking from the blast and with the help of the other campers, I able to stand taking a few steps to the picnic table where I sat as one of them patted my hot red forehead with cool water. I could hear someone kept saying I needed a doctor.

Now that question woke me up as much as the fireball that knocked me off my feet! Going to the doctor meant less time camping and trout fishing! I forgot how many times I had to say, "Noooo doc…tor, nooo doc…tor…" Now here I was a burnt to a crisp zombie and I am having a heated argument raising my squeaky voice to the point of yelling, "No, no,no,no…doctor

I shielded my face from the hot glow coming from the lantern on the picnic table which was giving off way to much heat for my fried face, assuring everyone again, I was not in need a doctor! One camper was so adamant about calling 911 that he even got me a mirror so I could see for myself the scorched face and all. Yes, I didn't look so good with my new hairless face lift and red glow in the dark complexion, yes, it did hurt, but I was still not going to the doctor!

The red glow tree embers were still popping and cracking with a real concern among the campers if the campground was still safe or will a fire start up.

I was slowly came out the blast daze listening to all the campers fears and opinions on what had caused the explosion in the first place; underground gas escaping from an old mine, trapped methane gas from old decaying dinosaurs, a pocket of natural gas left over from when Mt. Lassen was an active volcano…. Then they turned to me and asked what I did to create the blast? I told them, chocking on my dry mouth, that all I wanted to do was cook my rainbow trout for dinner, using paper and sticks to start the fire when it just blew up.

These good campers had all the right intentions by trying to get me to a doctor. All I really need was some peace and quiet and I even started to doubt if I was going to get that as the campers started to get to know one another. In a matter of minutes the campers decided to have a party and were suddenly scattering back to their campsites bringing over a ton of food, baked beans, corn, potato salad, barbecue chicken, a regular pot luck feast spread out all over the table! Only one problem, I couldn't eat! My lips were fried off my face! I felt like I was half dead and now here I was in the middle of a party! Everyone was having such a great time I don't think anyone notice when I left the table, open up the back of the camper shell door and climbed quietly over the tail gate shutting the door behind me falling lifelessly down on my sleeping bag.

This was one of the most sleepless nights I have ever had. Even though it was freezing outside the camper, I was burning up sweating gobs of perspiration as if I were in a sauna. My head felt like a flaming red hot marshmallow or a comet ready to explode. The rest of my body had no feeling what so ever, except for my stomach, it was growling for food, trout food.

I tried to get out of the charcoal crisp clothes, but the pain was killing me. The more I tried to moved, the more my body reminded me of how much excruciating pain I was in. The only energy I had left was to open my mouth to breath and let the sweat drip off my beet red colored forehead.

After a long restless night, the bright morning light finally peered through the camper shell windows on my third day of vacation, my growling stomach started thinking of the trout dinner I had missed. As I moved my dry cracked lips back and forth they began to bleed dripping big drops down to my flannel shirt and I wondered if I could eat anything at all. Slowly, moving my aching body, I proceeded to peel the charcoal crisp long sleeve shirt off my arms. Luckily, my jeans were only singed to a crisp in a few places, mostly the knee's, thinking it would be best to change all my clothes just to get away from the smell of burnt crispy flesh.

With a change of fresh clean smelling clothes I was feeling much better, "What a way to start a day! At least I was alive!"

Turning the handle on the inside of the camper shell back door automatically sets the air pistons in motion which pushes the door straight up in a quick swish. Taking in a deep breath of fresh clean pine scented icy air made all the difference in the world, facing another beautiful pine forest view, even if the view of the tall trees around the fire pit were blacken to crisp and still smoldering.

It wasn't long before I was climbing over the tail gate stretching my arms with a big yawn feeling so much better knowing I was still on a trout fishing vacation and not laid up at some hospital somewhere.

Looking around for what happen to the trout I was going to cook in tin foil, leaving it on the picnic table wondering if maybe one of the campers cooked it at their campsite, I notice a few bear prints around the picnic table and over by one side were little pieces of tin foil scattered about. In a deep voice I pretended to be a waiter taking Mr. Bears order at a fancy restaurant, "One well done cooked trout, for one big bear please, coming right up." Than Mr. Bear would say, "wait a minute, I've change my mind and will have the special, one well done blacken trout fisherman!"

I guess I was lucky the bear was not interested in cooked trout fisherman sleeping in the back of a truck or I would have been in the bear's stomach digested by now and coming out the other end!

Staying far away from the fire pit, in case the other campers were right about the cause of the blast, I started thinking about breakfast. Which would be easy because all I had to do was boil water for coffee, throw a couple eggs in for boiled eggs, a few slices of bread, not toasted of course because of my crispy lips and that would be it, breakfast done, "man, my burnt skin hurts!"

Shortly after finishing my light breakfast, the Park Ranger stopped by after hearing from the other campers about the fire ball explosion shooting up into the air. Calling me over to the truck window he asked if I needed a doctor for the burns, I explain to him that my first aid kit had burn cream and I was more shook up than anything else, reassuring him that I was a fast healer. Also letting him know the last thing I wanted to do was to end up in a hospital miles and miles away from a good trout fishing spot.

After a quick look over and apparently satisfied with his physical examination that I would survive, the ranger stared back at the fire pit shaking his head back and forth, "Nope, the explosion could have been from an old gas leak from an abandon gold mine shaft but its not, could be methane gas long left over from prehistoric days but it's not. Nope, I know exactly what made the fire ball and it happens more times than you think. A thoughtless camper had some liquid camping fuel left over but didn't know what to do with it. He definitely did not want to bring it back home with him so what does he do with it? He poured the gas into the fire pit thinking it would eventually evaporate. Now this is what happens, another unsuspecting camper goes to light a fire and Ka-bam! Luckily no one was too seriously injured or the forest didn't catch on fire. Remember to always approach a fire pit cautiously, you never know what someone camping before you threw in it."

With those fine words I learned something new, always approach a fire pit cautiously or you and your trout dinner may end up being burnt to a crisp!

As the Park Ranger was putting the gearshift into drive, he told me he would check on my healing process tomorrow, pointed to where the nearest phone was in case I needed to call 911 and waved good-by.

Since I looked a bit funny with a swelled up black scabby face, singed off eye brows, a newly half hairless black bald head and bleeding crispy lips which I could barely talk with, I decided it would be in my best interest to stay another night to heal up a little, even though I wasn't planning on it.

Another night without fire in the fire pit was doable. After all the fishing was good, that is, if I had any good luck left.

As luck would have it, I didn't catch a single yummy fish all day and ended up relying on my trout reserves in the ice chest for dinner.

While cooking a fourteen inch trout on the safe non exploding gas stove, listening to a Steller's Jay squawking for a morsel of food from someone's campsite, I started to think of what I enjoyed most about camping; the peace and quite would be the highest on the list, just kicking back looking at the different views and, watching the clean mountain air rustle through the tall trees tickling the pine needles is a nice added touch. You have lots of time, in no particular hurry to do anything at all. Just relaxing the day's away, day dreaming of anything that might pop into your head, like trout fishing.

Taking long walks along rippling trout streams is also high on my list, where in every step the forested landscape changes from enchanted meadows to thick skinny tree dense woods as you walk on cushion pillow of pine needles. If you're lucky, a special flip flopping rainbow treat will end up in your frying pan by the end of the day. "Yep" I love camping.

Flipping the sizzling fish to the other side I started to think about "luck," and I remember reading about some witch doctors in faraway lands recommend hanging dead chickens around your neck to ward off evil spirits. The witch doctors believe the evil spirits are the real enemy that caused you the bad luck in the first place.

I just couldn't figure out how carrying a smelly old dead chicken around your neck is going to change your luck, surly it's not a good way to meet new friends who just might be able to change your luck.

When I was a young kid, it was good luck to carry around a white rabbit's foot. Although, I could never figure out how carrying around a body part from an animal could help you. Besides, I would think the rabbit would want its paw back and the rabbit is now the unlucky one hopping around on three feet. How does making an animal unlucky, make you lucky by carrying around its foot?

My little episode with the fire pit explosion was not about bad luck or at least I thought that at the time, I was thoroughly convinced accidents happen and I just picked the campsite of a careless camper. On the contrary, I actually felt pretty lucky the fire pit explosion hadn't killed me, started a catastrophic forest fire and I had plenty of vacation time left to trout fish.

Now for a trout fisherman one of the hardest things to do is to decide "where" to trout fish? And it seems like every time I pick a place to go trout fishing I often run into my friend the big bear. Somehow the two just seem to go together, I fish for trout, hungry bear fishes for Danny McGee the trout fisherman. Why? Because Danny McGee the trout fisherman usually has delicious mouth watering freshly caught trout a hungry bear just can't resist.

That evening I sat at the picnic table shivering around a brightly lit lantern sipping a nice cup of cold chocolate next to a cold flameless fire pit and stared down looking at another one of my most prize possession sought after by many a fisherman. I keep it safe, well hidden, protected in three inch white water proof plastic tube, my "trout fishing treasure map."

What is a "trout fishing treasure map" you may ask?

Why trout fishermen search the world over looking for secret trout fishing spots. Some fishermen spends weeks, months, even years planning fishing trips and spending thousands of dollars on special fishing guides in order to catch a few trout.

And that is exactly what it is, a map that holds the treasure of trout fishing spots around the world. One of its kind; comprised from hear-say fishing stories and honest words of mouth secrets that only fisherman share. A treasure map worth millions, sought after by wealthy fishless trout fisherman everywhere.

My New Zealand trout fishing adventure is recorded on the map, Whidbey Island trout fishing, Rocky Mountain National Park backpacking trout fishing trip are recorded on the map, Montana, Idaho, Washington, Canada, Sweden, Switzerland, hundreds of trout fishing places all over the world are all included on the map.

Some of the best places to trout fish on the map are easy to find, others are so hard to find you just might not find the fishing spot at all unless you tromp all over the wilderness and half the world looking for it.

The map is as old as I am, first started when I was a young whippersnapper after being wounded by a fishing lure at Silver Lake. It is made of a thick white stiff yet flexible cloth material. When unrolled, you first looked down upon its thirty-six inch by thirty-six inch large size and see a rough drawn world map separating countries by water. Different color dots sprinkle the surface locating large cities, rivers, and lakes. Homemade cloth labels with hand written little notes are attached by a thin thread or fishing line. Baby pins hold other messages in some sort of secret code and only its owner, a fisherman named Danny McGee could decipher.

Flipping the map over to the other side is a more detail map of the United States, Canada, Mexico, showing all the main roads, lakes, rivers, creeks and streams going in every direction in different lines of colors looking like a big colorful plate of spaghetti. And just like the world map on the other side all sorts of funny looking objects and notes dangle from it.

Because of its large size, there was still plenty of room to make new notes on the map and that is exactly what I planned to do writing in large letters with a permanent red ink pen, "Hat Creek, watch out for exploding fire pits!"

Having fished in this area of MT. Lassen in Northern California so many times I probably didn't even need to check the map out but I wanted to be sure I didn't miss one secret spot where the streams were overflowing with rainbows, browns, brook or golden trout.

The next mornings on my fourth day, as soon as the sunlight started to peak in between the trees, it was time to say my goodbyes to the fireball camp site and the other snoring campers. With renewed vigor, trying not to think of all my painful ailments, I was ready to hit the road after a nice lukewarm cup of instant coffee and a yummy leftover cold Hat Creek trout sandwich on soft white bread.

My trout fishing destination for the next couple days would be driving and camping south on highway 89 stopping at as many good trout fishing spots I could find, including the big blue, Lake Tahoe, keeping a careful watch for exploding fire pits and the hungry bear.

As the days passed I really thought my luck had changed but it hadn't. I did not catch one trout out of any of the many creeks or lakes I had fished in, not on day five, day six, or even on day seven!

Not at Lake Almanor where I actually have a secret fishing spot to the north. On a certain part of the lake it is as warm as a bath tub because of a thermal hot spring bubbling up from the bottom of the lake attracting hundreds of big fish. I didn't catch one, not even a nibble. Or the Feather River, where just last year I caught my limit of sixteen inch trout everyday!

I knew I was having bad luck when at Donner Lake I was fishing on the shore and could see another fisherman maybe twenty feet away using orange floating power bait rolled up as a salmon egg, the exact same thing I was using and guess what? He caught fish after fish and I did not catch one!

At Lake Tahoe I rented a boat and was out on the cold water by 5:30 am with the fish jumping about all over the lake. I used everything in my tackle box, fly's, minnow lures, salmon eggs, earth worms, red worms, fake worms, fake crickets, fake shrimp, and all sorts of other stuff but did I catch one? No. Did I see other fisherman catching fish on the lake? Yes. I was tempted to just hit one over the head with an oar! At 5pm I finally gave up.

A whole week had now gone by of my fishing vacation, and the only fish I was able to catch came from Hat Creek!

The skin on my face was peeling off in chucks and I was starting to get a rash from using the public restrooms. I even started to think that I might as well go home but, one of the laws of being a true trout fisherman, or fisherwoman, is to never give up! A trout fisherman survives all types of severe natural elements, sheets of pouring rain, winter snow blizzards, fishing in mountain frozen streams, magnifying glass scorching heat, mosquitoes the size of dragon flies, hungry bears, lions, rattle snakes and all other sorts of discomforts. The Trout Fisherman's Code No. 1 says, "A trout fisherman never gives up fishing for trout until he has caught at least one, his limit, or until the trout have stopped biting."

That evening, I figured it was time to take closer look at my well hidden treasure map again, like I always do most every evening. Laying it out on the campground picnic table, I could see the outline of the eastern side of the

California Sierra mountain range. One place jumped out of the map giving me quick slap across the face saying, "Wake up! There are fish just waiting to be caught! What are you waiting for?"

The melting snow of the Eastern Sierra Mountains flows down into lakes, rivers and endless trout streams, to places like Scenic Bridgeport where some of the best trout fishing in the world can be found. I could spend more than one life time fishing this area, or two, or three, or ten or twenty lifetimes.

Being a trout fisherman, I often think about how I really could use maybe three, four, or even five life times. Just then maybe, I would be tired of trout fishing, but I doubt it.

Ah, but what is this on the map, a brand new reddish green sticker with a note on it folded in the shape of a little arrow that probably came off a watermelon pointing to a blue river line.

Looking closer, reading the details on the back of the sticker, I could see the secret spot was located on the Merced River and the directions told me it was not going be the easiest place to find. Next to the tiny red arrow was a smaller black arrow pointing directly at a curve in the river. The instructions on the watermelon sticker, as best I could make out the secret code read, "One car diet turn out, hike forest south west, 1+ mile."

"One car diet," meant you could fit less than a car in the pullout for parking. Not good because I had a truck.

Now I remember this one from my fishing buddy Jim, who called telling me all about this great trout fishing spot just as I was cutting into a big watermelon. Must have been about three years ago and I haven't talked to him since then. Hopefully, a bear didn't get to eat a trout fisherman.

Wow! This was great! It wasn't Bridgeport but I was excited. A new trout fishing spot on the Merced River that flows out of Yosemite! My luck was sure to change now! California's crown jewel Yosemite National Park with its breathtaking scenic vistas of mountain high towering waterfalls pouring over shear granite cliffs, rivers flowing through grassy open green meadows and miles and miles of endless hiking trails right around the corner. Yosemite has never let me down for hiking, trout fishing or just plain relaxing.

One person who loved Yosemite probably more than anyone else, the great hiker, camper, explorer and one of the saviors of Yosemite, John Muir who once said, "It is heaven alone that is given away."

At first morning light on day eight, I started driving towards Yosemite with such enthusiasm; all sorts of happy memories of camping in Yosemite years back were popping into my head.

One of those memories I want to tell you about happened when my wife, my five year old daughter at the time, she's much older now, and myself were camping one summer in Yosemite. One morning my daughter could talk about nothing else except going fishing in a lake that was a short hike from our campsite. Saying in her matter of fact little voice, "I'm going to catch dinner for everyone tonight!"

With a laugh I said, "That's great! What are we having for dinner?"

"Dad," She replied with a stern voice, "Fish of course!" I had to hide my laugh because she was so sincere and I wondered what she could be thinking of. She has never been serious about trout fishing before.

At the lake, my daughter pointed at a spot on another part of the lake and told me to go fish over there because she didn't want me catching all the fish she was going to catch for dinner. I was OK with that and a bit confused. What could she be up to? All she had to fish with was a little kids fishing pole, a thick rope for line and can only cast the huge plastic hook out about four feet in front of you. I offered to tie a worm around the end of the hook but she just told me to go fishing where she had pointed to. "I need to concentrate! Now you go over there!" she pointed.

My wife stayed with her as I did what she asked and went fishing on another part of the lake. After about an hour I headed back empty handed and I could see my daughter was still casting her line out and reeling it in. Not seeing any trout I ask her, "Well what's for dinner?"

Looking back over her shoulder after a cast in a matter of fact tiny five year old voice, "Can't you see? Fish sticks!"

I couldn't control my laughter, "Fish sticks?! Well I hope you catch a lot because I'm hungry!"

She said excitedly, "Oh, this is a really good fishing spot; we need to remember this place!"

And looking in the water that was exactly what she was fishing for, fish sticks! Well, sticks. Of course in the imaginative mind of a five year old girl every single one of those wood sticks floating, or sinking, in the water probably looked just like a frozen breaded fish stick you buy at the store. As a good mom and dad, we picked up all of her slimy fish sticks hooking a few on a stringer and brought them back to the camp site. There we pretended to cook them on the grill saying how good they tasted when they were done. What a good fishing-girl she was, later she made us promise that we would have fish sticks on every camping trip and never tell anyone about the secret fishing spot. She also made me put her secret fish stick spot on my fishing treasure map!

Thinking of the fish stick story brought a smile to my face and loneliness to my heart missing my little girl who is a very grown up girl now.

Day eight of my fishing vacation, the plan, driving down the forest mountain highway 89 turning onto the 88 highway in the morning, then down to the dry sage brush low lands going through the gold country picking up highway 49 in the afternoon, cutting back up into the Eastern side of the High Sierra Mountains via the 120 that will take me up the Merced River and into Yosemite before dark.

I would rather take the 89 dropping down to the eastern side of the High Sierra Mountains catching the 395 highway and fish Bridgeport cutting back over Tioga Pass to the Merced River, but if the pass closed because of snow, then I would have to back track all the long way back north to Tahoe to get over the pass to get home. That might take days.

Driving along it didn't take long to picked up highway 88, I hope to take a quick break at Kit Carson Lodge on Silver Lake and later stopping at the historical gold mining town of Jackson by lunchtime. That was the plan. Listening to the hum of the truck engine keeping my eyes glued to the twisting and turning of the mountain road, I tried to get some music on the radio but no radio stations were coming in. I cleared my mind of all other thoughts and open it to those old memories remembering back to an encounter my friend had with a black bear in Yosemite National Park.

One time I lent a very expensive backpack to a college buddy who was going backpacking in Yosemite for the first time. I told him about my some of my bear encounters in Yosemite and he said I was making them all up, just trying to scare him before his trip.

Coming over to my house just returning from his little backpacking outing, the first thing he did was to start apologizing all excitedly anxious to tell the story while holding out a bunch of twisted aluminum tubing in front of him, "I'm sorry, very sorry. We were hiking up a trail and this big black bear, I mean really, really big bear came running up the trail. We started running and the bear was gaining on us fast and seeing how I was the last one on the trail everyone started yelling at me to drop my backpack! As soon as my backpack hit the ground the bear was all over it ripping the material to shreds with his big claws. Then he used his big teeth to chomp down on anything that even looked editable including the tubing! He couldn't get into the bear proof container knocking it around all over the place. We all ran up the trail yelling to the top of our lungs back at the wild bear but the bear didn't even look up until he was completely frustrated trying to get into the container. And then, when the big bear did look up, we were all so afraid it was going to eat us next, we all took off running! When I had a chance to look back to see how close he was chasing us, the bear had actually turned around and was heading back down the trail. After I picked up what was left of the backpack we all got together and thought of the poor hiker going up the trail who will be facing that big unhappy hungry black bear. There was nothing we could do, we felt so helpless."

As he finished telling his story, I pictured in my mind meeting a big grizzly bear while hiking up a trail and before I could say anything the big grizzly bear gobbled down an innocent unsuspecting trout fisherman, me.

"Hey, I'm really sorry about your backpack, just tell me what it cost and I will give you the money, I'll write you a check right now."

I just looked at my friend with a smile and said, "And you didn't believe any of my bear stories?"

Sometimes that's what it takes to become a believer; you just need to have your own scary experience with a wild bear.

After remembering how my college buddy had such good luck with the bear that didn't eat him, only my back pack ended up with the bad luck, it started to remind me of other people who have had good luck during a bear encounter, or bad luck. It all depends on how a person perceives the outcome.

Good luck, because the person is still alive to tell the story or bad luck, because the person who had the experience of a close encounter with a big wild bear probably soiled their pants and might have a permanent scars including a few body parts missing.

Remembering to concentrate more on the winding mountain road I stopped my reminiscing mind so I could pull off a big layer of crispy skin from my cheek given to me by the fire pit explosion. I held on tight to the steering wheel with my one hand as I slowed into the curve a bit too fast screeching the tires. Lesson learned, I slowed way down, after all I was on vacation no hurry no worry as they say in Fiji "Singanalinga."

I was really hoping my fishing luck had change and I would finally end up with some trout to catch in the Merced River.

Flicking the big piece of bloody black skin to the trucks floor, my old memories started up again, as I started to once again think about luck. It reminded me of a time back when I was a young boy of seven years old, my dad loaded the whole family into the station wagon for a big camp out during our Thanksgiving school vacation at Sequoia National Park in California. In those days there were no bear lockers or little camp stores or flush toilets at the campground just open land and a picnic table. To feed seven people on such an outing we needed a lot of food which amounted to five boxes of stuff and I forget how many ice chests but one did have a big Thanksgiving turkey in it that my dad was going to cook on a spit over the open fire.

To this day I can still remember exactly what happen. I had my head out the car window enjoying the warm fall weather staring at the tops of the green giant redwood Sequoia trees as my dad pull into and back out of one campsite after another directed by my mom unable to make up their minds. Not until my baby sister started squirming and screaming for a diaper change drowning out the arguing did my dad pull into a camp spot on the outer edge of the campground next to a large grassy meadow.

Everyone is excited to finally be at our destination after what seemed like a ten hour drive. My dad was not the kind of person to let his kids just go run about and slap a few trees with a stick after he stopped the car. Nope, everyone had to help or you just might get slapped with a stick yourself.

So everyone had a job to do unloading the car and staying out of my dad's way. He was already busy carrying the heavy ice chests to the picnic table.

Our job was to get the tent out, sleeping bags and all sorts of odd ball stuff. That didn't last long as us four boys started punching each other and were put in time out in different places around the car. Eventually our mom and dad thought it best for everyone to help start making sandwiches with no shenanigans or dad would drive us straight home. None of us boys wanted to do another ten hour drive and immediately did what we were told.

And there we sat, all excited to be in the great outdoors eating our monster sandwiches with coke-o-cola and potato chips when my mom, who was trying her hardest to shovel baby food down my baby sister mouth, jumped up from the picnic table yelling in a you're going to die kind of shriek that only a mother could make, "BEAR!!! GET IN THE CAR NOW!!!"

My dad didn't think it was a big deal; he turned half way around to see four big black bears coming from the meadow running right for our camp site, shrugged his shoulders, took another bite of his sandwich and slowly started to get up. We were all following mom's orders piling into the station wagon crawling over one another not wanting to be the first one to be eaten by the bears. My oldest brother, the smart one so our parents told us, started trying to kick us out of the car yelling, "Eat him! Eat him!" My mom turned around from the front seat and gave him a good wallop on the head with my sister's glass baby bottle.

My dad was yelling to anyone who would listen, "Which box has the pots and pans?!"

I don't know what was more exciting, watching the lump the size of an egg form on my brother's forehead or watching my dad out the window who now had a pot in one hand and a frying pan in the other banging them together moving towards the bears.

By now, the black bears were all over the picnic table eating what was left of our delicious sandwiches. My dad had no urgency at all banging the pot and pan casually around the bears as if this was the right thing to do when you encounter a bear. Each bear weight over three hundred pounds, except one who was at least five hundred pounds, my skinny dad were only about hundred and seventy pounds making a very uneven match if the bears did attack him. But the big bear had other ideas, completely ignoring my dad knocking over the ice chest with the turkey in it onto the ground then trying to eat the whole bald raw bird in one bite. That was funny and entertaining. The other bears spilled out all the other crates of goodies and they were going to have a

Thanksgiving feast with all the trimmings, sweet potatoes, dressing, cranberry sauce, corn, green beans, and fresh bread. I was going to miss the pumpkin pie and ice cream sitting on dry ice the most of all.

My mom started to worry about my dad getting so close to the bears rolled down her window and started yelling franticly for him to grab the one ice chest the bears haven't knocked over that had the baby food in it and get in the car! Reluctantly, my dad did what he was asked and after my dad got into the car we all stared out the windows looking at the happy bears gobble up all the food.

I was really amazed on how easily a bear could open a can of cranberry sauce by stepping on the back of the can letting the entire contents squirt out in a liquid stream with the bear trying to lick up as much as big pink tongue could catch.

After the bears finished eating all of the food, including the turkey that the biggest bear ate in four bites and wouldn't share with any of the others, they circle the station wagon sniffing the windows until my dad started hooking the loud horn. Maybe that was the only thing my dad needed to do in the first place was to just honk the horn! As soon as they heard the loud noise the bears immediately stopped what they were doing and ran as fast as they could up the meadow disappearing into the forest.

My mom was not going to camp in bear country or even get out of the car to survey the damage and orders from her to us kids was the same, we were not allowed out of the car either!

Our disappointed dad picks up what he could salvage, crated the mess the bears made from the Thanksgiving party shaking his head mumbling something that us kids were probably not suppose to hear anyways.

We left the campsite with my brother who kept feeling the lump on his head saying, "Ouch!" every time he touch it, my dad still mumbling something about bears, my mom was taking care of the milk my little sister just threw up on the baby blanked covering her shoulder and me and my other brothers looked out the car window holding our noses from the stink. Orders were to not roll the windows down in case a bear wanted to jump in and if you even dared say anything about the stink, believe me, you would also end up with more than one lump on your head!

In what seemed like a three hour drive, up, down and around many mountains, my dad found a little cabin on a nice lake which met the approval of our mom. The resort had a little store that was still open and our whole family was happy again after we cooked some canned beef stew on the old black iron wood stove.

Although, we were all told that my dad could not afford to buy a whole turkey with all the trimmings again, because of the cost of the cabin and all, at least we would have turkey sandwiches made from package turkey tomorrow on Thanksgiving Day. We didn't care, the only thing us boys couldn't stop talking about were those four big black wild bears!

That night my dad kept saying, "Of all the bad luck, of all the bad luck…" I think I fell asleep with that sentence in my head while sniffing the nice pine scent of the cabin all snuggle up in my sleeping bag barley noticing how hard the floor was. It must have been 2am when my dad was shaking us kids awake, looking up I could see a bright orange glow in the cabin. My mom was looking out the window holding my baby sister who was fast asleep in her arms. My older brother was asking, "What's going on, what's going on?"

My dad said in a very calm serious voice, "It's a fire; the cabin across from us is on fire and you three boys need to get up and help with the fire brigade, try not to wake up your younger brother."

I looked around to put on my clothes and realized I had slept in them needing only to put on my shoes, which just happen to be already on my feet. I was up and ready to go.

When my dad opens the cabin door I could immediately feel the hot air blow in coming from the burning cabin totally engulfed in red hot flames just four car lengths away in front of us. I had never seen such a horrific inferno fire before, completely amazed and stunned at the roaring fires strength. I watched in horror the power of flames completely devouring the small cabin bellowing enormous clouds of black smoke into the night sky.

The night was now completely lit by the fires orange glow. We followed my dad out of the cabin into the parking area closer to the intense heat of the fire storm. I could see a long row of men, some shirtless, handing buckets of water as fast as they could to one another starting from the lodge up the road.

Only when we came closer did I see another single file line of women and kids, like myself, taking the empty buckets after the water was tossed to the burning cabin bringing them back up to the lodge completing a full circle.

One of the men in line saw my dad coming and pointed to where he would be needed, towards the front. He made another hand signal to a lady in the line behind him waving again for us to hurry up. Without stopping the momentum of the passing buckets, pots, pans and anything that would hold water, we went through the line and were quickly placed in the empty container brigade. I never new how fast my arms could go and after a short while how even the smallest container without water could feel so heavy.

All night long the cabin burned until the sun came up finally giving way to smoldering black embers and a long over due rest to my arms that felt like they would fall off. The lodge staff wanted to say thank you to everyone by giving everyone a free pancake breakfast for helping put out the fire because the lodge and all the cabins could have also burnt down as well if it wasn't for the bucket brigade

Over breakfast, everyone was talking about how lucky the people were who were staying in the cabin that caught fire and were able to get out in time before the fire got out of control. Someone said the fire was started by the people trying to slow cook a turkey overnight in the wood burning stove oven, the stove got to hot igniting the turkey grease in the pan catching on fire sending huge flames shooting out of the stove setting the cabin on fire.

The people from the cabin were too shook up to join everyone at breakfast, getting a room at the lodge from what some said, so I guess until someone can ask them know one will know.

For some reason, my dad never told anyone at breakfast how we lost our turkey to the bears, but I told every new kid I met that day and they all wished to see a bear eat a turkey in four bites!

During our Thanksgiving dinner that evening, while enjoying my paper thin slice of turkey in between two slices of white bread at the little cabin table, I figured I learned something very important in life that day. If you are having a spell of bad luck with four big hungry bears, someone else out there in life is having a lot worse bad luck maybe even escaping out of a burning cabin. There is absolutely nothing anyone can do about it except for looking at the situation as good luck. My dad did not get eaten by the four bears, even if he was asking for it, and the people in the burning cabin got out in the nick of time to live another day, "You can't get any luckier than that!"

Once again feeling a burnt crispy scab itch on my chin, waking up from all those old memories listing to the hum of the engine looking out at the beautiful mountain landscape whizzing by, I couldn't help but wonder if bad luck was still following me.

ANSWERS TO CHAPTER 2 QUESTIONS

a. This could be absolutely true! The black bear is in his natural habitat and could care less about you because he has not been a people condition bear. (A people condition bear is one that is used to eating human food.) Move slowly to the side far away off the trail as possible from the bear preparing for the worst scenario and let the bear pass keeping a sharp eye on him and remember all bears are unpredictable!

b. It's always nice to have friends to go backpacking with to protect each other but now let's say none of your friends could go and you have decided to go alone. There you are having a stare down with a big black bear who hopefully only wants what is in your back pack. If you were smart enough to pack everything in a bear proof bear container than you're in good shape, as long as the bear isn't hungry enough to eat you!

Now you can go up the trail or down the trail, going in another direction off the side of the trail is an option if the trail is not steep and you think the bear is just going to its berry patch. Here again making lots of noise use an air horn if you have one and just maybe the bear will turn around walking away. If the black bear is determined to take your backpack its always better if you're not in it!

Move far away from the bear and if you want to live dangerously stand there watching him rip to shred every item in your back pack. When the bear is finish and you have decided to live dangerously go pick up the pieces. It would be a good idea at this time to watch your back because the bear might just claim your property as his now and if he is still hungry the backpack was just an appetizer and you will become the main course!

If you decided to not live dangerously try to think of all those survival skills you learned sitting on the couch while watching TV and now is your big chance to put those skills to good use as you make your way back to the trial head.

C. This is the best solution; only a crazy black bear would try and confront four humans with bear proof containers, air horns, mosquito sprays, cooking sprays, yelling, screaming, but what if you need to confront four bears at once?

Having a plan on what exactly you're going to do when you encounter a bear, or four bears, along with all the information about the bears in the area before you hike, is just good common sense.

CHAPTER 3

*("Hey Grizzly bear, I see you tip toeing around
trying to sneak up on a trout fisherman!")*

What would *you* do?

You are up in the high country sleeping alone in small tent, suddenly you are awakening by grunting and sniffing sounds from a very large animal. Under the light of the moon you watch the dark shadow slowly walk around the tent, then stop, turn his head putting his large snout against the thin nylon material pushing it in slightly. You shake in horror as you watch a sharp claw easily cut through the tent material and a big bear paw reaches in.

A. Lie perfectly still, not making a sound, crossing you fingers the bear does not succeed in finding the candy bar you took to bed just incase you got hungry in the middle of the night.

B. Jump up yelling and screaming to the top of your lungs slapping the big hairy bear paw that reached inside the tent and say, "How dare he wake you up! This is not the time for bear games!"

C. Pee in your pants and tell yourself, "Life is over as you know it."

YOSEMITE'S TENT CABIN BEAR SCARS

Keeping myself busy picking off a few more itching scabs above my eyebrow driving south of Lake Tahoe passing a few empty ski resorts on highway 88 I knew very soon I would be at the top of Kit Carson Pass at 8650 feet elevation with Silver Lake just on the other side. Childhood memories started bouncing around in my head thinking back on all the good times I had at Kit Carson Lodge playing shuffle board and fishing in the Lake.

After reaching the summit, and even though I had a long drive to the Merced River, I just had to stop to wet a line in Silver Lake. But I had to be very careful, like a magnet I could be pulled right into the Alpine surroundings for the rest of my fishing vacation.

Finding a good turn-out I stop the truck grabbed my gear anxious to catch a fish. The lake scenery was just beautiful, cobalt blue sparkling lake surrounded by thick green fir tree forest with a background of snowcapped pinnacle granite mountain peaks. First using worms then red devil spinners I gave up after an hour disappointed of not even getting a bite but typical of the way my fishing luck was going. It didn't help that the Merced River kept popping into my head, telling me to quit wasting precious time and get on the road!

Driving down to the low lands I always get the feeling of having forgot something I left in the mountains, it wasn't the fish I didn't catch I forgot, it was a part of me that wanted to stay. My intuition kept telling me I was going in the wrong direction. Intuition is sometimes very confusing.

As usual, when driving long distances, instead of listening to the radio I open my storage mind of long ago memories, the third eye thing, thinking back to an old memory with regard to having good luck, or bad luck, on a past trout fishing vacation.

Many people in Yosemite have this good luck, bad luck thing going on, especially if they stay in one of the many tent cabins.

Yosemite's breathtaking natural beauty attracts hundreds of tourist looking for peace and tranquility. Some may just find it, if they are not being chased by one of Yosemite's bears!

Some people say the park itself is being loved to death by too many visitors. I guess that's true especially in, "Yosemite Valley," where visitors stay in hotels, lodges, wood cabins, canvas tent cabins, or campgrounds which are completely full most of the time.

Yosemite National Park also has something to offer everyone. There are short hikes to waterfalls, long hikes to waterfalls, hikes to grand views, hikes through grassy meadows, hikes along rivers and creeks and you can hike the back country backpacking to Little Yosemite Valley or to one of the many pristine alpine lakes. You can also climb sheer granite cliffs if you're a rock climber, ride bikes on one of the many trails if you're a bike rider, fishing is always good, the water perfect for summer swimming in one of the many rivers or lakes. Or you can just be a lazy head and hang out, relaxing, doing absolutely nothing enjoying the scenery.

For the first time tourist visiting Yosemite and meeting up with one of its famous bears is the furthest thing from their minds. That is until nightfall. It's not the imaginary boogie man that comes out and you can turn on a light to scare him away, uh, ah. This one is very, very real, has long sharp claws, is very, very hungry and will eat anything that even remotely smells like food with their large dagger teeth.

Sometimes I like to stay in the rustic tent cabins at the canvas tent village in Yosemite Valley, nestled among the pine trees, if I am not lucky enough to get into the campground. They call it a Village because they offer all sorts of accommodations and kid activities, a swimming pool during the summer, a large food pavilion, a pizza place, and a small store for groceries and tourist things.

Part of the village includes newer wood siding duplex type one story hotel rooms with a small deck. The small cabins are, well, old wood sided cabins and some of them have bathrooms. The rustic house-keeping duplex type cabins are located down by the river and have an open three sided fenced patio. They do not have bathrooms.

My brother likes house keeping cabins best because he can store all his river floating gear in the fenced patio area. He can also cook or barbecue all of his meals outdoors.

Like me, he doesn't think it's a big deal to walk a little ways to use the bathroom, and like me, he sometimes gets a hot shower. My brother often tells me, "House keeping cabins have never had a bear problem because if a bear did show up, everyone at house keeping would grab their pots and pans and make so much racket the bear would high tail it right back to the tent cabin village where you're staying!"

He still believes the best way to get rid of a bear is to make a bunch of noise with pots and pans. I sure hope he never runs into an aggressive bear!

I like staying at the tent cabins because it reminds me of how John Muir and the other first explorers of Yosemite lived in the valley. The tent cabins are located under towering granite cliffs and from time to time even a few large boulders the size of a car have fallen down, but I don't think anyone has been killed yet.

It's a full on tent neighborhood hidden among the tall canopy of pine trees. No cars are allowed, the only way to get around is walking the rough small dirt paths crisscrossing around gigantic granite rocks and pine trees.

The tent cabins themselves are made up of a dark green painted "A" frame wood structures which is covered by thick white canvas tent material. From years of rain and snow the once white canvas is now discolored in a dirty off white color with a few brown smudges. Most of the tents are built right next to each other in long rows, but some of the tent cabins are sitting right on top of the granite boulders and others are like tree houses with a long stairway going straight up to them.

You get a lockable thin wooden door in a forest green color with a window screen on the upper half, two screened windows with a canvas shade operated by a pull rope, one bare sixty watt light bulb which hangs in the middle of the room operated by a pull string, two or three cots consisting of a pillow with case, two sheets and one thick scratchy army blanket. If you're lucky, you will also get a small desk and if you're very, very lucky you will get a canvas tent that only has one or two bear ripping canvas repair scars.

What are bear ripping canvas tent repair scars? First time visitors don't have a clue unless they ask someone. And even if they ask someone I don't know if that person would tell them the truth wanting them to find out for themselves if they don't follow the rules. But I will tell you all about bear ripping canvas tent repair scars.

Everyone who registers to stay at the canvas tent village must sign a paper saying they have read and agree to the all rules, including using bear lockers for food storage big enough to put an ice chest in, no food in cars that sit in the parking lot overnight and absolutely no food in the accommodations including toothpaste! But usually only one person registers, signs the rules while thinking how to handle the entire luggage situation because the parking lot is a long distance away. The other's in the same entourage are giggling over maps and rushing off to the village store to buy candy bars and souvenirs, completely clueless about the dangers of wild bears.

Yosemite Park Rangers warn everyone at the entrance to the park about the black bears in Yosemite; it's listed on the hand out flyers with the park map telling everyone not to keep food in your cars but to use the bear lockers for ice chest storage at night and all food items, including perfumes and tooth paste. Under no circumstances should you ever feed a bear! It's a death sentence for the bear! But does every one listen to the park ranger or read the flyer?

It is a very important policy not to have wild bears looking at humans as a food source. If wild bears did start to see humans as a food source, then soon they would begin to look at humans as a fast food take out and will start aggressively tearing us humans apart looking for a morsel of food. At some point, wild bears could start seeing humans as food and depending on how hungry the bear becomes, this could lead to a bear eating a trout fisherman, hiker or tourist on a daily basis.

Now black bears are very unpredictable, as any bear expert will tell you, (*I am not a bear expert, just a trout fisherman),* and if someone comes back from Yosemite with a bear story, especially if it has to do with bear ripping canvas tent repair scars, it's more than likely true, because it did happen to them!

It is understandable to think that a few people are not being properly informed, somehow forgetting to read all the information about the bears information handed to them when paying the entrance fee into the park, or forgetting all about the rules because they are overwhelmed by the Yosemite outdoor experience.

They also forget all about the candy bar in their coat pocked left over from the hike, keeping the jacket close to them on the bed at night in case they get cold.

This would be the ultimate mistake! This would give an open invitation to any hungry bear out on his nightly walk that is looking for a small treat.

These hairy giants of three hundred plus pounds are fierce creatures that are armed with sharp teeth and claws that can rip a car door off its hinges!

And yet, only in Yosemite this fierce hairy creature carefully tip toes in the dark of night, sneaking around the canvas tent village sniffing out any yummy treat. Once the scent of the yummy treat has been found inside the canvas tent, the bear ever so cautiously takes one sharp nail, and ever so silently, makes a rip just big enough to get his big hairy paw inside. He is usually so quiet that nobody inside the tent wakes up from hearing the canvas being torn.

Now, seeing on how it is very dark inside the tent, and bears do not carry flashlights, the bear's paw with the sharp claws feels around the bed looking for the hidden mint flavor or chocolate treat. No matter how cautious the bear is, the bear paw always finds a solid lump under a blanket and he knows exactly what it is. But since he has a one track mind he does not care one bit about the lump under the blanket, he keeps telling himself, "I can do this, no one will wake up. It's going to taste so good..." That is when he might get a little too anxious, sticking his big hairy head inside with all of his sharp teeth.

Some tent cabin visitors think its best to lie still and not do or say anything when confronted with by a big bear paw on top of them in the middle of the night. Or even when the paw goes under the blanket searching around and the visitor gets poked a few times by the bear's sharp nails. But fear instincts tell most people to scream at the top of their lungs in complete hysteria, as if the bear had already taken a large chunk out of them. This works every time, no bear wants to stick around and listen to bunch screaming maniacs.

Gee, I can hear the tourists now, just like I have heard it so many times before when I was sleeping in the tent cabin next door. Woken up in the middle of the night by a tourist franticly yelling to the top of their lungs as if a bear is truly eating them! "BEAR!!! BEAR!!! HELP!!! HELP!!! A BEAR IS ATTACKING ME!!! BEAR! HELP! HELP!"

Then the kids wake up and start yelling and crying. The whole entire tent neighborhood wakes up and is now in mass hysteria. Everyone is scared out of their wits thinking a bear is in their tent! When the lights are finally turned on the neighborhood realizes the bear is not in their tent and the parents can be heard trying to calm down the scared and crying children.

But the tourist who had the bear paw under their blanket is not calmed down at all and is curled up in a ball screaming their head off, still convinced the bear is outside the tent and ready to come in and eat them. By now the other neighborhood guests are outside with their flashlights looking up and down the dark bumpy paths for the bear hoping to get a glimpse of it forgetting all about the traumatized tourist that encountered the bear.

Not finding a bear during the ten minute search, realizing only then of what would they do if they did find the bear, the neighborhood search party decides to go back and examine the tent with the newly ripped canvas, where the bear reached his paw in attacking the tourist.

After hearing first hand from the tourist that was attacked by a bear paw, the search party figures out the bear was only after the toothpaste that must have been forgotten on top of the bed because its gooey mess was now covering most of the green scratchy blanket.

The shaken tourist is unconvinced the bear was only after the toothpaste, not remembering the candy bar still hidden in their coat pocket, vowing not to sleep another night in the canvas tent. Telling everyone who shared the tent to pack their suit cases! They were going straight home!

Now the traumatized tourists will be scared of bears for the rest of their lives seeing the situation as bad luck and it's all because they forgot about not putting their toothpaste away in the bear locker. At least they will have a good bear story to tell when they get home and lucky for them, the bear decided not to come completely inside the tent to see what else he could find!

What many tourists don't realize is that when they do not follow the rules with regard to bears they are putting a death sentence on the bear and maybe human being. The bear will be coming back again and again, looking for sweet smelling tasty toothpaste, a candy bar, or anything that even smells remotely editable. And when he does come back, he just might not be nice and friendly, and run away but stay to eat a tourist.

The next morning, after canvas tent village management hears about the bear incident, and no, you won't get a refund if you invite a bear into your tent cabin as a guest, a maintenance person comes over putting a long piece of bright white waterproof repair tape over the ripped canvas. The new white tape does not even match with the existing weathered canvas material that has faded over the years. By 5 pm new happy tenants will arrive and move their entire luggage into the tent cabin not having any idea of what happened inside the night before.

Like most tourist, they probably won't even ask about the Yosemite tent cabin repair scars and hopefully, if they don't want a visit from the big hungry Bear tip toeing around in the middle of the night, they will have read and plan to follow all the rules, double checking their pockets before going to bed and will have a good night sleep, and just maybe, so will I!

On this long drive on highway 88 going towards the town of Jackson, I was now concentrating on picking off more scabs on the top of my nose hating that fire pit explosion, while trying not to run off the winding road squealing around the corners. My old bear memories were moving right along and I started to remember back to a time when I actually saw someone in Yosemite get a free bear ride.

ANSWERS TO CHAPTER 3
QUESTIONS

a. Do you have a choice? That big black bear with all those razor sharp teeth is going to be on top of you in a matter of seconds looking for that candy bar! Slap that bear paw and yell to the top of your lungs as if your life depended upon it, because guess what? It does! The bear might not be after the candy bar at all, he might be after you as a midnight snack!

Never bring food into your tent unless you're planning on having a hungry bear in the middle of the night as a guest!

My daughter once met an eleven year old outdoorsy girl, camping at Lassen National Park who would wake up and go trout fishing all by herself at 5:30 am and swim across Summit Lake before 9:00 am. She really wanted to see a bear and had absolutely no fear of them. Every night, she would put scented perfume products around her tent to attract a bear! Lucky for her, a bear never did come by to visit!

b. Even if you don't have a candy bar and a black bear has decided to come in. Jump up, yell, scream and hopefully you are prepared with an air horn and some sort of spray! After all, you are sleeping in bear country!

c. Well what did you think was going to happen when you planned on going into bear country unprepared? The bear was going to give you a big bear hug and playfully snuggle up in your sleeping bag with you

CHAPTER 4
FREE WILD BEAR RIDES IN YOSEMITE?

("I tell you the other bears were wrong, trout fisherman do not taste like trout!")

What would *you* do?

A big black bear has just walked into your campsite while you are making breakfast. The bear completely ignores you and starts devouring everything on the picnic table.

A. Hurry and get the kids for free bear rides?

B. Yell and scream at the top of your lungs and bang together anything you can get your hands on to defend your territory? Or is it the wild bear's territory?

C. Run and lock yourself in the car if you have one, or salvage what you can without disturbing the bear and stuff it in the bear proof container as fast as you can hoping the bear is only interested in your breakfast and not you!

Free wild bear rides in Yosemite did I say? Now that's an old memory I will never forget, or my old friend Jake and all the good times we had together. Although, I reminded myself to concentrate the curvy road or I would end up just an old memory! And I reminded myself again to lay off the itchy scab pulling! The town of Jackson was less than an hour away which should give me enough time to remember most of the story before stopping for lunch.

The bear ride event happen back when I was a single college man taking every chance I had to get up into the mountains and go trout fishing! Most of the time when on a fishing trip, I camped out in the wilderness somewhere, or in a campground. Since this fishing trip involved fishing around Yosemite with a college buddy, Jake, who was lucky enough to get a campground reservation, our first night camping is one I will never forget.

After a long hot summer day of trout fishing and hiking the dusty switchback trails to Vernal and Nevada waterfalls, Jake and I decided it was time for a hot dinner meal back at our "Upper Pines" camp site. Walking pass other campsites along the way, we could see the other campers had the same idea, as smoke from crackling campfires spewed out of fire pits, smells of hot dogs, baked beans, hamburgers, carne asada, and spicy chili filled the air. Little kids ran around in every direction under the watchful eye of parents who held bubbly drinks while chattering away with new neighbors. Riding bears was the furthest thing from anyone's mind, except for maybe one person.

These were definitely good family times, camping under the pines trees in Yosemite. For us, it was two good avid fishing buddies who were able to take some time off college and explore the back trails of Yosemite.

We were also hungry, starved, wanting something fast and easy. Fast and easy meals were canned beef stew or canned chili with a can of corn on the side, canned salmon with a side can of peas, or canned something and of course rainbow trout wrapped in tinfoil to go along with our canned delight. It would have to be out of a can because as long time campers we both knew fast and easy usually meant whatever was in the can could be cooked right over the camp fire. The dishes were fast and easy too. You only need to wash one spoon or fork. If you were still hungry, you just opened another can of something.

While enjoying our dinner, out of our many cans, picking bones out of our teeth from the rainbow trout, we looked over to the other campsites seeing that most of the kids had inhaled their dinners and were jittery waiting for the camping encore. The kids were not the only ones who felt the excitement. Grownups with happy faces ripped open plastic bags shouting, "Marshmallow time!"

Neither Jake nor I had forgotten about the fun either of cooking a nice, perfectly warm golden brown marshmallow over an open fire. After all, we had to have desert even if it didn't come in a can.

Now there is definitely an art to cooking a fragile, lightweight soft marshmallow over a burning pit of red hot wood coals. I have yet to meet a connoisseur who loves to eat a marshmallow that has just caught on fire, looking like a red flamed comet from outer space. Or anyone who might enjoy a burnt out red flamed comet that has turned into a blackened crispy expanding bubbling gooey melting mess by the fire.

Most people just toss the burning ones back on the fire creating a smoke bomb blowing out in every direction chocking the very air of all the marshmallow cookers. But that doesn't stop anyone to grab another fresh one, that is, if there is another one. Once the marshmallow desert frenzy starts, it's a free for all to see who can eat the most in a shortest amount of time, including eating them just the way they are, powdery, soft and chewy.

Let's not forget all those campers who love to eat smores! I know some people who don't even like smores, saying, "Why take a big piece of chocolate, a hot marshmallow sandwiching them in-between two graham crackers? Who needs the graham cracker? The best way is to take a perfectly cooked golden brown marshmallow, dip it in nicely melted bowl of chocolate and wool-la! The best, sweet delicious snack you have ever had. Yummy! Some campers don't stop just at chocolate dipping a many include caramel, butterscotch, nutella, peanut butter and any other concoction they can think of.

Campfire dinners with fancy marshmallow deserts filled the air sending the scented smoke high above the tree tops into the valleys over the high granite cliffs down hidden canyons and hideaway caves where the biggest local residents live, the wild bears.

Every evening, not too far out in the woods a relaxing black bear would start his usual ritual of picking up the scents of treats with his long nose from unsuspecting campers. The bears probably know the scents by heart from all the take out restaurants being a return customer after scaring the campers away from their dinner, hot dogs, hamburgers, barbecue chicken, canned beef stew, canned pork and beans, all coming from down in the campground valley below. Also probably wishing some forgetful camper will leave an ice chest out at night filled with bacon, eggs, steaks and all sorts of goodies for a feast beyond a black bear's wildest imagination.

Some bears are interested in handouts from people, others bears are just interested in "taking." Which one of these bears, a non-aggressive or very aggressive, will show up at your campsite and what will happen depends entirely on how a person has prepared their campsite.

If a person is diligent about keeping the bear proof container door shut after taking something out, then they do not have much to worry about. If they didn't, and a hungry bear shows up, get ready to go shopping again.

And of course the bear has no interest in you because you have prepared yourself with loud pots and pans, yelling, air horns, etc.

My personal experience of camping in Yosemite Valley is not if the big black wild bear will show up, but when! And maybe not just one! Campers should always be ready for more than one bear to walk into their campsite at anytime in bear country.

Jake and I finished our own ritual of stuffing ourselves with marshmallows and after dousing the camp fire with water it was time for an evening campground walk.

The summer sun was slowly setting sending golden streams of light through the pine trees creating outlined shadow patterns on the ground. Nature's final light show to end the day was just beginning.

Jake and I were in absolutely no hurry, slowly strolling down the black asphalt listening to the chatter of campground life pointing out the most entertaining, some older kids huddled around the fire pit trying to see who could make the biggest flaming marshmallow comet, throwing them up into the air then landing on the ground in a big loud "splat!" Still others were running around wild pretending a bear is chasing them having the time of their lives.

It's always fun to check out all the license plates on cars, to see where everyone is from; Georgia, Maine, Oregon, Nevada, Arizona, and a rental car from New York. People have come from all over the place to enjoy Yosemite's Natural Wonders.

This is also a time to check out what kind of camping gear people are buying; cabin tents, small and large dome tents, three room bubble tents, tents so big they look like circus tents taking up the whole campsite. One campsite had even put up a three foot fence around the perimeter!

Walking passed the last campsite on the end of the loop we notice all the campground chatter had disappeared. The sun had gone down, dusk was upon us now and the thick forest of pine trees grew tall on both sides of the road casting dark black shadows on the ground.

I really don't know who first saw the wild bear casually walk out of the dark forest but we both froze like statues. A young small black bear under 200 pounds stopped on the pavement for about a minute. He held his nose high and sniffed the air as if to confirm the direction of the sent before starting to walk down the middle of the road. He was walking away from us and of course we had to follow.

From behind, we could see the hairy bear move from the middle of the road to the left side. He was heading back to where campers were still busy with nightly chores under the bright light of lanterns. We lost site of the bear completely a few times hidden under dark tree branches. The bear was completely camouflaged by his black fur coat silently moving in and out of campsites sniffing unsuspecting camper's tents, looking under picnic tables, for any morsel of food.

We continued to follow the bear as he made his way back on the dark pavement sniffing the air for scents that were of interest to him. A tap on my shoulder made me turn my head towards Jake who was pointing towards a campsite right next to the road, "Hey, look over there, that lady has spotted the bear."

Yep, she saw the bear alright. First she started looking around to see if anyone else had seen the bear. They hadn't, and she didn't spot us standing on side of the road because we were hidden by the dark shadow of the trees.

We could also see her three year old little girl enjoying herself eating a marshmallow at the picnic table. Wondering what the lady could be up to when we saw her quickly grab the little girl around the waist, lifting her up, securing the child to sit on the side of her hip. She looked around, then reached out and put something else that was on the picnic table into her coat pocket. She reaches out again grabbing a loaf of bread off the table. Taking a final quick look side, to side, she started walking as fast as she could in the direction of the bear.

We watched the lady briskly make her way around a few pine trees headed right for the bear, bouncing the small child around like a rag doll.

We watched in disbelief as she walked right up to the wild bear, which was completely startled at first and started backing up, until the lady turned the bread bag upside down shaking out the white slices to the ground.

For the bear it was all about food. He didn't seem to mind a hand out from an over confident camper. What happen next made our mouths drop! The lady took the small child from her hip, and set the child on bear's back! She took a step back, pulled out a camera from her coat pocket and took a picture with her flash!

Jake I both started screaming at her to get the kid off the bear!

I thought the bear would take the kids head of in one swipe but it didn't and I can't tell you why. It was the strangest thing I had ever seen.

The bear had now inhaled the bread and the lady shook out more from the bag not giving it a second thought the kid might get injured, all the while taking more pictures!

Jake and I started running yelling at her to get the kid off the bear!

We tried to grab the kid off but the lady kept blocking us forcefully pushing us out of the way! Frantically we screamed at her that the bear could kill the child! It's a wild animal!

Finally, the lady grabbed the kid and yelled at us, "They shouldn't have bears in Yosemite if they aren't tame!"

Now, I thought I had heard it all. No more bears? Unless they are tame enough to put your kids on their backs to take a picture? Hey, I know just where the lady can go to get a picture of her kids on top of a bear. Take highway 1 to Northern California until you come to the Klamath River where you will see two full size golden bears on both sides of the bridge. Now I wouldn't recommend putting your kids on those bears and taking pictures because of the traffic on the bridge. However, if you keep going north to the town of Klamath, you will find two life size golden concrete bears that are made just for putting your kids on their backs to take pictures. You can also get a picture of your kids standing next to Big Foot's Grave!

Other campers who saw the camera flashing and hearing the commotion started to gather around taking their own pictures of the bear, who was now looking at all the people waiting for another handout.

The Yosemite Park Ranger soon arrived, "All right people give the bear some room, let the bear move along." Even the bear knew this drill, he turned and ran right back into the dark forest.

Jake and I did the same, continuing on our nightly walk through the dark forest among the sparsely lit glowing campfires.

I felt very lucky walking back to our campsite, lucky for the kid who didn't get injured by the wild bear and lucky the bear didn't turn on us, but luck has a funny way of changing real fast and the night was not over yet.

Now I had done it, I pulled a big giant scab off my lip and its starting to bleed profusely. I tried to reach into my back pocket for my handkerchief to stop the bleeding but the truck swerve to the left, I over corrected turning the wheels to the right running off pavement into the dirt, I turned back left swerving onto the pavement gaining control. "Whew," that was a close one; thank goodness I didn't fly off the cliff!

The itching of my scabs along with the long lonely drive was starting to get to me, as I tried to figure out how much further I had to go before reaching the historical town of Jackson, where some of the richest gold producing mines were located. "Mmm, searching for gold or searching for the elusive trout? That's easy, catching a golden trout would be perfect!

ANSWERS TO CHAPTER 4
QUESTIONS

a. Now does that really sound like a good idea?

b. Yelling and screaming at the top of your lungs, use an air horn, bang together anything you can get your hands on to defend your territory is probably the best idea, and just maybe the bear will become so annoyed he just leaves. Bears hate loud noises.

c. But what do you do if the black bear has decided you are encroaching on his domain by staring right at you, getting closer making loud grunting sounds, his ears are folded forward, and he doesn't care one bit about the food?

If you had a car it would be a good idea to get in it and start driving.

Make lots of noise, yell, scream, make yourself big standing on top a log waving your arms, use an air horn, throw things around to make more noise, anything to let him know that it's your camp and you plan to defend it! Throw things around to confuse the bear there might be more of you, and let's put it this way, your life might depend on it!

If you are backpacking and all you have is a tent set up with all of your food in a bear container, then it would be a good idea to leave everything and slowly walk a long, long ways away from the bear crossing your fingers he doesn't follow. Maybe you can go back and retrieve the bear container later, but don't go back thinking the bear will just disappear because he is after something and plans to get it!

Or you could spray him with anything you might have handy but from what I have heard from fellow backpackers is all that will do is make the bear really mad. Now you have an angry bear more determined than ever to fight his aggressor, although, this could be your only option, giving you a little time to get away.

This might be a good time to leave everything behind and brush up on your survival skills you learned sitting on the couch watching TV, as you make your way back to the trail head.

CHAPTER 5
MAMA BEAR

("Hello mama bear, cubs? What cubs?")

What would *you* do?

Driving along you spot a big mama bear with two small cubs in a forest meadow munching on some brightly colored flowers, "What a great picture," you say to yourself.

A. Get out of the car running up to the bear as fast as you can for that special once-in-a lifetime close up photo. (Best way to make a bear mad)

B. Stay in the car, reach your arms out the car window and take the best picture possible.

C. Get the bears attention and share your picnic food with them.

I was in the town of Jackson just long enough to fill the truck up with gas, stop my lip from bleeding and also wanted to get something to eat in town, from what growling in my stomach was telling me, but ended up only getting a milk shake because of the condition of my scabby lips.

It would have been nice to go to the museum and check out all the mining equipment they used to get the gold out with reminding myself not get sidetracked. I was on a mission to get fishing at the secret spot on the Merced River driving the fastest way to highway 49 turning east to the 120 going towards Yosemite.

As usual, getting tired of listening to the loud static from the radio station signals, the movie player in my head starts up going right back to where I left off, back with my friend Jake camping in Yosemite.

When all the commotion was over with the Yosemite bear rides, Jake and I moved on to finish our nightly walk around the campground. A bright full moon started to ascend above the black tree tops, sending white streams of moonbeams through the dark trees, lighting up the whole forest as if it were daytime.

Walking by campsite, after campsite, we could see all the campers had quietly settled down, sitting around dwindling camp fires, kids snuggled up in their parents laps talking in low voices, some were singing old campfire songs and others were reading from a book telling scary ghost stories.

The light of the moon lit up our campsite that was just ahead and looked just like any other campsite except for one thing. It was a blemish on the neighborhood, a run-down structure that reminded you of something that should have been demolished long ago. Burning it down would have been a favor to other campers. The smell alone made campers walking by hold their breath and accused each other of farting. There it barely stood in all its past glory, Jake's decrepit old cabin tent, with its multi dull colored ugly stains, leaning to one side, looking as if it was going to collapse at any second.

That embarrassment of a thing should not even be in the same class of even being called a tent, more like a torture chamber, definitely not a tent. It should have been thrown away long ago and would have been if it wasn't for the sentimental value attached to it. As with many sentimental items being passed to the next generation that maybe should never have, the tent was handed down to Jake from his camping dad who now lives fulltime at an elderly care facility unable to participate in camping any longer.

The memories of past camping trips while sleeping in that tent were the only thing of value. Jake could go on and on forever, reminiscing back to all the good times with dear old dad, who was nick named Burt Reynolds because he looked so much like Burt Reynolds the movie star. Along with dear old dad their old dog Fred, a large shorthaired mix of who knows what, always came along.

The tent had traveled to the Grand Canyon, Glacier National Park, Yellowstone, the Smoky Mountains, Appellation Mountains, to just about every State and National park on the U.S. map. Jake even still had his dad's old wood panel Mercury station wagon handed down to him with a blown head gasket now forever parked in their backyard. It doesn't run anymore, but looks better than the tent. They used to take it on all those trips collecting decals stickers of all the places they stopped at plastering them all over the windows.

If you ask Jake what all the black and moldy looking stuff in big blotches covering different parts of the tent was, he would tell you in his deep down home bull frog voice becoming so excited that you even asked, "Oh, that's just old dried up spots of mildew straight from the slug capitol of the U.S.A., the Olympic National Park Rainforest in Washington State. Now let me tell you about that camping trip!"

"Burt Reynolds…," Jake used to always call his dad Burt Reynolds because he wanted other people to think that his dad was a movie star. The only problem was that no one knew who Burt Reynolds was anymore because he is now such an old movie star, "…and I were driving along somewhere in the Olympic National Park in the early morning fog and slid right off the road, just missing a tree. Do you know why? Because there was so much slime left over from the hundreds, no thousands of yellow banana slugs that crossed the road everyday! The hardest part of walking down the sticky slimy and messy road to get help to pull the car out, was trying to stay on your feet! Constantly we were slipping and sliding, one foot this way, then one foot the other way, trying not to fall into the gooey green slug slime. I had the gross stuff all over me, mostly on my hands from picking myself up and slipping again getting stuck in the slime glue. I couldn't even spread my fingers apart, and my backside was black and blue from hitting the pavement so hard. It really hurt having both my feet slip right out in front of me into the air landing on the hard asphalt in a thump. Ouch!"

"On top of that, I had a feeling, with so much sticky slime on the bottom of my pants, that at anytime I would slip and fall becoming permanently stuck to the road like chewing gum!"

"Finally, we were able to get to a small campground, with a little store down the road, where they sold slugs on a stick, but were really just chocolate suckers shaped like slugs. And the store had all sorts of banana slug stuff, including slug jam, slug butter, slug pens, slug hats, and slug t-shirts. After the nice man from the store pulled our car out of the ditch, my dad liked the campground so much, because it was close to hiking trails and fishing, that we decided to camp for three nights."

"Every morning we would wake up to a drizzling wet fog that brought hundreds of yellow banana slugs moving about. At one point, there were so many, they completely covered our tent! The tent itself took on the appearance of a bumpy, yellowish brown funny looking sculpture. Every inch of the tent canvas had a banana slug attached. When it came time to take the tent down after our stay, we had to borrow a shovel to scrape them all off!"

"After we return home, my dad didn't even try to get the slime off the tent, saying it was nature's natural way to water proof."

When Jake first told me that story, I remember asking him, "So Jake, what you're saying is that all those banana slugs only left slime on your tent and that caused those big black looking blotches? I think they left something else behind besides just slime."

Jake would never let me get the best of him, "Now Danny, you have been to the Olympic National Park and know perfectly well it's a rain forest and nothing can stay on your tent very long because of all the rain. Hey, did you know every time we go camping in Olympia National Park, we stop at that same little store to buy a yummy slug on a stick, and run up and down the road slipping and sliding all over the place? It's a blast! You really need to go up there and try it sometime."

Jake usually starts telling story, after story, never shutting up, talking about his great hand me down tent. How it has protected his dad, him, and the dog Fred, through so many unbelievable snow storms, wind storms, sand storms, lightning storms, and all sorts of other storms including a soap storm. Yep, even a soap storm. That's a good one.

It came about when they were coming back from a camping trip and found themselves driving out in the middle of nowhere on a windy night. Jakes dad became tired of dogging tumbleweeds flying all over the place, deciding to take one of the many dirt roads going off into the hills. One dirt road split into two dirt roads, up hills, down into little valleys when they finally come to a stop, not having a clue where they were.

Trying not to get blown away while setting up the tent, Jake remembered telling his dad the place smelled like soap and he was getting covered by white dust. His dad said he didn't care, and just wanted to get some sleep.

All night long the white dust collected growing an inch thick all over the tent. Right before morning it started to drizzle from a wet fog turning the dust on the tent into a thick white gooey paste.

After a long restless night, Jake woke at first light wanting to find a bush to relieve himself, stepping outside the tent he saw the whole ground covered with tiny soap bubbles. Coming back from the bush he couldn't help but smile, seeing the tent as one giant vanilla ice cream cone!

When they were ready to pack up, Jake and his dad both argued saying it looked big white frosting cake saying, "It can't be an ice cream cone because it doesn't have a cone!' and Jake saying, "A scoop of Ice cream doesn't always need a cone!" and on, and on,…

Taking down the ice cream cake tent didn't help with hot tempers as the sticky substance was like glue, making it impossible to fold up the tent correctly. Even their gloves stuck to the tent, so eventually the tent was dragged to the back of the station wagon and just pushed in.

Only after they drove back to the main road did they see the sign that said, "Welcome to the Borax soap mines, tours by appointment only."

Now you would think Jakes tent would be clean as a whistle after they hosed it off at home, but on the contrary, the opposite was true. The soap that blew on Jakes tent was not refined, or diluted, and was in its completely natural state, a strong chemical. So strong, the soap stuck like glue to the tent and was almost impossible to roll out and set up once they got home. His dad spent hours diluting the glue with water to pull the tent apart before he could set it up again. Finally they let the white layer that was left on the tent dry in the sun, slowly curing into a black icky, sticky, foul chemical smelling layer of filth.

After a few days Jake and his dad were very proud of their new and improved tent, the glue had completely dried to a solid form now making the once canvas material indestructible from any harsh environment. It was a tent made almost entirely out of white glue.

We both now sat on the picnic table staring at the leaning tower of yuck, under the bright light of the moon. I wanted to razz Jake a little because he was always relaying the history of the tent so seriously, one would think it had special powers or something.

Say Jake, "How many times did you say your dog Fred marked his territory on that tent over the past eighteen years? What, two or three thousand times? Is that what all those brownish yellowish stains overlapping in different places around the lower three feet of the tent are from? Hugh?"

"What about the time you were camping out in the back country of Mt San Jacinto when someone forgot to zip up the tent and found a scared skunk inside spraying in every direction? Did you ever get that smell out of the tent? And what about the time you were camping at Morro Bay and being the nice person that you are, decided to feed the seagulls until they started sending white bombs splashing down from the sky like it was hailing. You told me there were so many turds dropping that the smelly liquid was dripping down the sides! How many seagull bombs did you say? Around two hundred or more spattered plops over the three days didn't you say? And what about the time you were camping over by Prairie Creek campground, where you told me the only place to pitch your tent was on fresh Elk dung. How did that make your tent smell?

Or, the time you pitched your tent on a beach next to a sand covered log using it as picnic table. Only to realize on the fourth day of trying to figure out where a really strong dead smell was coming from did you discover the log wasn't a log at all but a large decaying sea lion the wind had covered up with sand! Didn't you tell me when you got home that the tent smelled like something died in it? Are you sure nothing has died in it? I know I would if I spent even one night in that tent!"

Jake just took it all in completely ignoring my observation of the condemned tent, so I continued, "And you're going to stink it up even more because all you had for dinner were pork and beans with a little trout! That means gas-a-rue, double stink-o! How you're going to survive the night in all the foul smelling air will be a miracle!"

Finally I was getting to him, I mean hey, what are friends for? Jake was starting to sound a bit grouchy, "Enough about the dang tent!"

I completely went into shock when he asked, "are you sure you don't want to sleep in my tent? It's all set up, you don't even have to put your tent up and you and I both know about those Yosemite bears."

Where did Jake go while I was telling him how his tent reminded me of a torture chamber? I guess he just tuned me out like you turn off a radio.

Looking straight at him, raising my voice a bit so he doesn't tune me out again I said, "No way, can't you see this is a once in a lifetime event? When do you think I would get another chance to sleep under the stars during a full moon in Yosemite Valley on such a beautiful warm summer night? It's so light out you don't even need a flashlight to see things!"

Jake shook his head while getting up from the picnic table and slowly walked towards the tent, what a health inspector would red tag and label,

"DANGER! CLOSED TO THE PUBLIC! HEALTH HAZARD! QUARANTINE! DO NOT UNDER ANY CIRCUMSTANCES PROCEED FURTHER!"

Jake reached up to unzip the tent, "Hey Danny McGee, what about the bears? Ever think a wild bear might come and eat you in the middle of night?"

I started laughing with a big smile on my face, "Bears don't scare a trout fisherman like me! I figure the bears are looking for food and as long as I am not food to them everything should be fine. Besides, I have backpacked all over the High Sierra's, Cascade Mountains, the Rockies, and I have never had a problem with bears. A porcupine wanted to eat me one time and a few skunks have given me some unpleasant memories, I've been attacked in the middle of the night by a gang of raccoons tearing my tent apart and trying to eat me, but never bear's."

As I watched him enter the death chamber, a bit concerned if he might not wake up alive, Jake in an insecure kind of voice says, "Well good night then, see ya in the morning."

Not wanting to part with Jake on a sour note after bashing him about his tent he loved so much, "Hey, it was a great day catching all those trout and wasn't that mom crazy for putting that kid on the bears back?"

At least I got a small laugh out of Jake before he turned in, "Yeah, a crazy lady, at least the kid didn't seem traumatized, good-night."

Watching Jake zip up the mangy tent, hoping he doesn't die in there, I started to feel a little sorry for him. It must get real lonesome camping without Burt Reynolds and reminiscing all the good camping times they had together.

Taking in a deep breath of pine scented clean fresh mountain air, feeling sleepy, I decided it was time to call it a day and started to make my way over to the car.

Opening the trunk I pulled out my backpack looking around for a soft place to sleep, definitely somewhere upwind from Jakes toxic dump!

We were very lucky to have camp spot with no neighbors on both sides of us, I guess they had a change of plans and could not keep their reservations. That made more choices for a perfect spot, picking a place on the very edge of our campsite, just incase the neighbors did show up at three in the morning.

As I have done so many times before, rolling out my sleeping pad onto a thick mattress of dried pine needles, under a few nice smelling trees. I reminded myself this was a gift that only a few people can appreciate.

Pulling a mummy sleeping bag out of my backpack, then shaking it to bring a little fluff up, I spread it out over the sleeping pad and started to think of what Jake said about the bears, "ah, what does Jake know?"

I take a good look around, to the other moon lit campsites that had already quietly settled down. Once blazing fires were now smoldering red glows, loud voices turned to whispers, bright lanterns from picnic tables had traveled inside tents. "Bears, I don't see any bears!"

Stuffing my boots back into the backpack, because I didn't want some scorpion, spider or snake, to make them their home in the middle of the night, followed by my shirt and pants, I pull the plastic lock on the top tight. With the end of the string I tie it to the top of my sleeping bag, knowing if some animal, like a porcupine, raccoon, or bear, tries to steal my backpack, I was sure to wake up, while either being dragged or strangle. I have been dragged and strangled by wild animals in the middle of the night realizing one again there has to be a better way, but I told myself I would figure it out tomorrow.

Moving a little faster, because my bare skin was getting cold fast, I crawled into the mummy bag feeling like a cocoon zipping it all the up way to my neck and stared up at a billion stars twinkling like shinny diamonds. I was in awe, watching a shooting star streak across the sky. Everything was perfect for sleeping under the stars. I lay all cozy in my sleeping bag smelling the fresh pine scented mountain air. It had been a long day of hiking, swimming and fishing in lakes and rivers you only see in travel magazines.

I was going to sleep good tonight and thank goodness I was far away from that smelly tent. Which got me thinking about Jake, would if he really did die in his tent? I felt bad. Hindsight tells me if I had a chance to save him I would and should. I really didn't want to deal with a dead Jake in the morning trying to explain that his tent killed him. I was getting worried about him suffocating. It would be easy to cut a hole in the top of the tent to let some of the gas out. Knowing Jake he probably wanted to smell the fresh pine air too and cracked a window. With that last thought, I remember falling into a deep long sleep.

But sometime woke me during the middle of the night, my eyes were sprung wide open, a feeling of fear shivering up and down my spine. Something with teeth was tugging on the bottom of my sleeping bag and something else with sharp teeth was tugging on my backpack above me. Not wanting to startle whatever it was I played possum. I didn't move a muscle staying very, very still, thinking it's just a raccoon and now I will have to get up and deal with it. Whatever it was, sounded like a puppy making growling noises, it started tugging harder on the material while pulling back, then started turning its head back and forth, "Grrrr…grrr… grrr…"

I could now hear small rips in the material. It was tearing my sleeping bag apart! I knew I was going to have to put a stop to this before the sleeping bag was so torn up and the next bite might be my flesh!

The plan, should I fight or flight? I decided to first take a quick look to see what I was up against. Rolling over, sitting up ever so slowly, peeking out of the small hole of the mummy sleeping bag, I saw what looked like two little well rounded puppies, with dark brown fur. I smiled and laughed, "How cute they were. Some kid is going to be pretty sad to find his two little puppies missing."

Moving my feet around in the sleeping bag to play with them a little, "Grrrrr," I suddenly heard a loud crash like a big barbecue was being knocked to the ground at the campground across from us. Turning my head around, I could see in the moonlight the outline of a huge, and I mean huge, at least 500 plus pound wild bear! One of the biggest bears that I had ever seen in Yosemite was standing on its hind legs turning over a heavy picnic table! I took another fast look at the puppies. They were not puppies at all! They were wild bear cubs! I knew I was in the worst position a human being can be in! Right between a mama bear and her cubs and mama bear sure sounded angry for not finding any food!

My underwear covered butt jumped out of that sleeping bag as fast as lightning and I ran right for Jakes tent, unzipping it as fast as I could with the two puppy looking wild bear cubs right behind me. I jumped into the tent trying to push the bear cubs out, while trying to zip the zipper down. The cubs started to whine like crazy alerting mama bear. When I looked up, mama bear was running to her babies at top speed. Scared out of my wits, and shaking like a leaf, I finally got the zipper down. But what good is this, I asked myself? All that separated me from mama bear's big teeth and sharp claws was a thin piece of old stinky canvas material!

"Hey, get off me! What are doing?" Jake said in a sleepy voice sitting up.

I was so scared, I could hardly talk. I tried to whisper, but coughed, unable to take a breath because of the heavy mildew and urine smell. I managed to stutter, "Bear…really big bear, not, a happy mama bear with two cubs."

I put one shaking finger towards my lips, "Quiet, shhh…!"

With a puzzle look on his face, Jake started to yawn trying to comprehend what I was telling him, "I thought you weren't afraid of bears?"

Jake laid his head back down to go back to sleep saying, "yah, its o.k. if you want to sleep in the tent."

There was no time to reply, putting my finger to my lips regretting I had even inhaled another breath, whispering, "qu…ite," then to my ears, "listen."

Jake somehow just figured out what was going on and quickly sat back up whispering, "bears?"

In the moon light, we could see shadows of the mama bear and the little cub's right on the outside of the tent. Mama bear grunting in bear language to the cubs probably asking the cubs if the human hurt them in any way.

I couldn't move a muscle, and one look at Jakes face told me he was scared to death too! We watched as the big bear slowly sniffed around the tent. Every now and then, she would raise her head and push her nose against the thin material as the little balls of fur squealed around her. I knew the wild bear was trying to decide whether to rip the tent apart. Her big nose and excellent sense of scent probably told her there was no food to be found in the tent, just humans, and I was really hoping maybe mama bear thought the old tent, with its heavy smell of pee and mildew, was so disgusting she did not even want to see what was inside. But then again, if she was really hungry, she just might put a few humans on her menu.

I stood like a statue holding my breath, dying from the stench and started to wonder which would be worse, to be suffocated by the tents methane gas or chased by a bear! I was getting ready to be chased by the bear, because I was gagging inside the musty old tent! Reaching down, grabbing the zipper, I watched the giant bear's head suddenly rise up. I thought it was over. She was coming in. Jake was still in his sleeping bag.

"Good luck, Jake." Feeling a bit sorry he was going to have to deal with a big mean mama bear.

To this day, I have never seen anyone move as fast as Jake did. He was out of his sleeping bag before I even finished saying, "good luck, Jake," and he was reaching for the zipper I had my hand on. Now it was a shoving match to see who could get out of the tent first and start running the fastest because the looser would be the hungry bear's meal!

With a loud grunt, a big sniff, followed by another grunt and two little squeaks, we both watched the three shadows slowly start to move away from the tent.

I couldn't move the zipper up fast enough, falling right out of the tent onto the ground, holding my neck gasping for air chocking from the toxic fumes!

Jake thought I was kidding, "All right, that's enough, get up, it doesn't smell that bad."

He thought I was kidding? "Oh yes it does!"

At a distance, I could see mama bear and her two cubs, going off down the road making their way to another campsite in the light of the bright moon.

Brushing myself off, Jake started insisting that I sleep in the tent, "I told you it was a special tent, and it even keeps away the bears! And come on, the smell isn't that bad."

Times like these, is when I realize some people really do have rocks for brains. Jake somehow completely blocked out everything I said about his tent.

"Ya know Jake; after I go pick up my stuff, I think I will just go sleep in the car."

The next morning we were eating breakfast at the picnic table and I wanted to tell Jake the real reason why I didn't want to sleep in the tent without him blocking me out again. As friends, I thought it is a good thing to be truthful even though you might hurt the person's feelings. I felt it was very important because I could actually see someone dying from the leaking methane gas fumes.

So for the next half hour, I drilled Jake again and again on why the tent should be retired to a good dumpster.

Jake didn't seem to mind at all, telling me he had seen a tent he really liked on our walk last night, "Yeah, my tent is so heavy and hard to set up and I really can't smell anything because of my allergies but now I have decided as soon as I get back, I'm going to buy me a brand new cabin tent!"

"So what are you going to do with the old canvas tent, and all those attached sentimental memories Jake?"

"I'll hand it down to my kids of course, just like my dad did to me and that's probably the biggest reason why I want a new tent, so I can save the old one for them. I will even tell them it has special powers to keep away big Mama Bears!"

I just about spit out all of my hot chocolate I was drinking, I guess good tents with all those memories and special powers just never die.

Closing my movie mind, after reminiscing back to all of those Yosemite camping memories, driving the long road to the Merced River, I was even able to switch over highway 120 all the while dabbing my bloody lip promising myself not to pull off any more huge scabs, I can't help but think of what the bears might have in store for me on this particular fishing trip.

I figured the camper shell should protect me from any bear waking me up in the middle of the night and seeing on how I didn't have any fresh trout I shouldn't have a problem with bears. Now if my luck does change and I catch a few out of the Merced River then I might run into a little problem with a bear chasing after my most prized possession. But usually bears do their thing and I do mine, so I told myself to stop worrying about bears and to start concentrating on the road and fishing!

Reaching up, peeling a thick scab off the tip of my nose, "Now what fly should I use first when I get to the river?"

ANSWERS TO CHAPTER 5 QUESTIONS

a. You might think this is a no brain-err, all you will have to do is run back to the car for safety after you took your photo. One thing is missing out of this picture, Mama Bear. And she doesn't care if you're in a car or not! If she decides you're a threat, then life will be over as you know it. Whether you live or die depends on how fast you can run to your car on the two skinny legs you have, with the bear right behind you on her four powerful legs. You will also need to open your car door, start your car and drive off. You might find the bear wanted to go for a ride and is in the front seat sitting next to you after she ripped the car door off!

Bears can run up to 30 miles an hour, how fast can you run in rugged terrain?

b. Da, safety first.

c. Feed the bears? I hope you have your affairs in order and have an updated will.

CHAPTER 6
ONE BIG HUNGRY BEAR FISHING FOR A TROUT FISHERMAN

("Have I seen a trout fisherman? Sorry, haven't seen one all day. Fishing pole? What fishing pole? Oh…, that fishing pole.")

What do *you* do?

One early morning, you and a friend start hiking up a trail in a beautiful National Forest known for its many different wild animals including the grizzly bear. Part of the trail brings you to a very thick dense pine forest and right in the middle, taking up most of the path, is a huge pile of brown poop with a steam cloud rising above it blocking your way. You realize right away that it came from a very, very large bear, and that he must be close by.

A. Turn around and find another trail in an entirely different direction.

B. Go forward further up the trail with no fear because you are prepared believing it's easy to face down a grizz and maybe get a close up photo of the bear.

C. Step in the very big pile of brown poop with both feet, squishing around back and forth, getting as much of the stink on you as possible, thinking it will take away your human scent and the bear won't find you.

Time was going by way to slow driving on this mountain road, thinking I drove around the same pine tree line corner on Hwy 120 ten times, everything was starting to look the same except my handkerchief, which was dotted with bright red blood stains. I just could not keep those nasty negative thoughts out of my head, so I started to wonder if my trout fishing luck had really run out forever, never to catch another fish again. Somewhere, somehow I drank an evil witch's brew, or a curse was still following me from the fire pit explosion, or a poltergeist was haunting me from the legendary, maybe living, maybe dead, ghost fish called, "King George."

I had a feeling it had something to do with King George and I can still remember back on how George got to be "King."

Many years ago, up at one of the Lakes in the June Lake Loop located on the eastern side of the Sierra Mountains in California, one of the tackle shops wanted to do something nice for all the trout fishermen. With all sorts of hoop-a-la they tagged a trout, naming him George, and a cash prize would be awarded to the fisherman who caught George. For every week George was not caught, the cash prize would increase.

Years and years have gone by and only an occasional fisherman has been able to hook George, who must weigh between four to twenty-four pounds by now. No-one really knows how much George weighs because the occasional fisherman was not able to get him into the boat. Many a fisherman came back with stories of a fish doing unbelievable acrobatic tricks, flipping, flopping, flying out of the water again and again, twisting, turning, and giving the trout fisherman a real show, including a quick glimpse of his shinny blue tag, before unhooking himself splashing back into the water.

The stories of fisherman hooking onto George can be heard in the tackle shops over and over, that is just one of the things that made George "King." What really made him King on the June Lake Loop was that George started showing up in all the Lakes, Gull Lake, Silver Lake, June Lake and Grant Lake. Yep, fishermen were hooking onto George in all the Lakes positively identifying the one and only blue tag just before he released himself from the hook. How is that possible? Trout fishermen were coming up with all kinds of hearsay ideas trying to figure it out.

Just when someone says King George must have died of old age by now, a fisherman reels him in only to get a another look at his tiny shimmering blue tag right before jump, turn and flip, unhooks himself.

Year's back, when I heard how much King George was worth, I dropped everything and headed straight for June Lake. I fished the June Lake Loop for days only catching tiny one's which I tossed back and no sign of George. As I was sat on a bench at Gull Lake, relaxing at the tackle shop enjoying a morning coffee while watching the aluminum boats cling clang bobbing around in the water, a weather beaten old trout fisherman came and sat down next to me. In a scratchy ex smoker voice, he leaned over to make sure I could hear him, "Its George yah know. Every year the trout get smarter and it's George who is doing it. No one at the tackle shop realized George was a special fish, intelligent. He tells the other fish if they want to get big and live forever like him they must not feed during the day, stay on the bottom, and only feed on the top of the lake very late at night when no fishermen are about."

Wanting to hear more, I asked, "Some fishermen are saying George has some sort of fish extrasensory perception and he is teaching the fish in other lakes how to escape a hook with aerodynamic twisting and turning. He's also telling the other trout to evolve growing extra bluish silver scales to look like a fish tag, same as his, just to show off all the other little Georges growing."

I wanted to tell him about the evolution of one species, the "Horned Lizard" that can not only puff up their bodies to look bigger but have evolved being able to shoot blood from their eyes to frighten predators. Or, the Malaysian ant that can explode as a defense mechanism whenever it wants blowing up everything around him to protect the rest of the colony, but I didn't think he wanted to hear about such things.

Getting a sense of hostility, the old trout fisherman stood right up shaking his head gritting his teeth, "That fish has cursed us all! Someone has got to catch that fish!!!"

As I watch the determined old trout fisherman walk away in a huff, I realized what the other fisherman told me was maybe true. Somehow King George's is projecting himself to the other lakes telling secrets about how not to get caught by trout fisherman. That has to be the only reasonable explanation for the bad luck I'd been having on this fishing trip starting with the fire pit explosion. Could the King George curse be responsible for me not catching any fish?

Yes, even a trout fisherman's mind can get a little delusional when deprived for a long time of using one of mans natural instincts, trout fishing!

Giving myself a quick slap in the face for a quick wake up to concentrate more on driving highway 120 before I ran off the road and there will be no more memories, positive thinking told me not to worry. With my handy dandy fishing treasure map this trout fisherman is not going to be without trout for very long.

But it's a funny thing about maps, even the fishing treasure map looking at all the bright color spaghetti lines going in all different directions, sprinkled with little black pepper dots identifying cities and towns, yet never really giving a clue of what your finial destination might actually look like.

Maps are good when they can give you directions to a certain place where you want to go and sometimes they are not very good when they give you directions you to places you didn't want to go, a roadmap of gibberish. Just because it's on the map doesn't mean the place, or road, actually exist. Trust me, or I might send you a map with roads on it and place that don't exist.

Believe me. I have been made a fool for believing a map more than once. Someone should make it a rule which says you can't make a map, unless it is guaranteed that every road is a real road and not an imaginary one.

Maps can be very misleading when a mile might feel like ten miles, "as the crow flies," it's just over the hill, and another hill, and around another corner, and around another corner, until you find yourself crisscrossing all over planet earth finally coming to where you wanted to be, or you are completely lost. And did you know the person who first actually draws the map puts fake towns and roads to identify it as their original work as a copy right. No wonder so many people get lost, even when a GPS reads the map.

A trout fisherman's treasure map is not any different than a regular map, well maybe just a little bit different, a little harder to read because it's in secret code and has no fake roads or towns. It is often compared to construction blue prints, which I found out long ago are only guide lines. Come to think of it, isn't that what any map really is, "Guide lines?"

Those same guide lines from the trout fisherman's treasure map finally brought me here to my destination, the Merced River, driving down the two lane road following the river looking for that one special turnout that probably did not even exist any more. Maybe a flood came by changing the course of the road, or a winter mud slide sent a whole mountain down completely devouring the road. Who really knows, it was getting late and I needed to stop to get some fishing done.

Eventually, I turned around and drove back up the road, turned around again and drove down the road finally giving up pulling off the road onto a small patch of dirt next to an overhanging cliff. It was my best guess to where the secret fishing spot might be located, according to the map. The butt of my truck stuck out into the road by just a few inches, maybe twelve.

Hurriedly grabbing my fishing gear, along with my winter jacket, I looked up at the orange glow in the sky through the thick tree tops realizing darkness would be upon me in a matter of one short hour.

Making my own trail through the thicket of the woods towards the Merced River I eventually came upon the fast moving white water making its way through gigantic granite boulders creating little water falls empting into deep swirling pools of crystal clear water. I could actually see five or six nice fourteen inch trout swimming around.

The secret fishing spot on the treasure map didn't lie. This was the spot described on the map! I caught a rainbow trout on the first cast using a barbless dry fly with little yellow-reddish wings and green tail. I just kept telling myself that my luck had finally changed!

When fishing is this good, the sense of time was the last thing on my mind. All I kept thinking about was catching more fish until I had my legal limit.

Long gone was the orange glow of sunset, it was getting darker and darker, I didn't even notice. The night sky had turned black but all I could think of was fishing, fishing and more fishing. I could not see a thing, except the glow from the white water in the river. All the standing pine trees around me become one black mass; I just keep fishing, and started to hope a bright moon would come up so I could actually see *where* I was fishing.

The fish were now not cooperating at all. It took hours before I finally caught the legal fish limit under the light of a half sliver of a moon. I started looking around the dark forest wishing I had a flashlight, thinking this might not have been one of my best ideas.

Of course, it would be easy to loose one's way under these circumstances, a dark thick forest between me and my vehicle. I was just too busy fishing down stream, jumping from granite boulder to boulder, zigzagging from one side of the river to the other, not paying attention to the darkness that is now upon me, and could leave me in a death trap. If I were to slip on a wet rock, and hit my head falling into one of the deep pools of water, I would certainly drown. But never fear, we are talking about the fearless super hero; the trout fisherman! He will always live another day just to go trout fishing, just a bit broken bruised burnt to a crisp or fishing in trout fishing heaven. (New Zealand)

Fishermen usually have a very good sense of direction. The highest peak in California, and the 48 contiguous states, Mt. Whitney at 14,490 feet was first climbed on August 18, 1873 by trout fishermen Charley Begole, Johnny Lucas and Al Johnson naming it Fisherman's Peak. They had no map or well marked trail. They just said to themselves, "The best trout fishing must be over that hill," so they hiked up that hill, "The best trout fishing must be around that corner," and around the next corner eventually hiking up so many hills going around so many corners they reached the top of the highest mountain in California. I wished they would change the name back to Fisherman's Peak to honor the superhero trout fisherman who first climbed it.

Now that I had my fish limit, tromping blindly through the night forest getting slapped and poked by every single tree branch I didn't see right in front of me, I felt as if I was fighting for every step. I tripped over logs, easily falling down, was getting strangled by weight of my loaded fishing bag strapped around my neck all the while trying my hardest not to break my fishing pole!

This little adventure was turning into a terrible nightmare and the worst part was I could not even imagine what direction I parked my truck!

Not only that, but I thought I heard something following me, fear shivered up and down my spine. I stopped to listen, listening hard beyond the light breeze rustling through the trees, I knew something was out there, I could feel it. Raccoon, fox, bobcat, lion, or bear?

Which could it be? No time to wait and see, I tried to not make so much noise, which was impossible making my way through the unforgiving thick forest. I stopped and listen again, fear was taking over me, and I needed to get ready to fight. My fishing pole and the heavy fish bag were my only weapons.

Two dark black eyes were watching me, I could feel it! Uh, oh, now I could hear him breaking small twigs with his heavy paws coming fast in my direction. He was after me!

Fight or flight, fear shivered up and down my spine raising the hair on the back of my neck straight up! It was not time to dilly dally any longer, the race to get away or be eaten was on! I started crashing, bulldozing through the bushy pine limbs at top speed, keeping my eye's shut and opening them only to get a quick bearing from the little light of the moon. I was just barley ahead of the big animal!

That adrenalin fear sensation of getting eaten by some Jurassic T-rex animal goes back to when I was a little kid catching my first rainbow trout at Silver Lake. After letting the trout slip through my fingers back into the water, looking up, and right there in front of me, was a big bear looking at me right in the eye. I could tell he was trying to make a decision for dinner.

Whenever I catch a trout, be it night or day, I always get a little sense of fear thinking a hungry bear's eyes watching me. Every time I wonder if the bear has made up his mind if he is going to eat the freshly caught trout, or is he going to have freshly caught trout fisherman!

Right now, I think the bear that's chasing me only wants to eat a freshly caught trout fisherman!

With my heart pounding, running as fast as I could blindly plowing through the forest with the bear right on my heels I kept telling myself, "Drop the fish bag, drop the fish bag, don't drop the fish bag, don't drop the fish bag." Over and over, "don't drop the fish bag, drop my fish bag, what ever you do, don't drop the fish bag!"

Just when I thought my luck had completely run out, the smooth asphalt road was under my feet and I could see the back of my truck was not that far away in the distance, with a quick look over my shoulder, "Yeeo!" I told myself to, "run faster, run faster!" The bear was picking up speed and I needed a plan now! Another car coming down the road would be a big help!

The truck was coming up and I knew I would not have time to unlock my door and get in. The bear would have me right about when I reached the door of the truck. Then an idea popped into my head like a light bulb going off! I knew one thing I could do, it was something that I had played when I was a little kid trying to get away from my older brothers and now I had no choice but to play the game with the bear!

Looking back over my shoulder again, I had just about the length of the truck between me and the bear which was all I needed, I thought. I ran passed the back of the truck, passed the passenger side door and came to skidding stop, facing the hood and looking down on the side of the truck for the bear. He was nothing but a black blob, not stopping his momentum for a second! I took off running around the truck with him following right behind me only now the bear had to slow down to make the sharp turns. So the game around and around the truck began. How many times I ran around the truck, I don't know. I didn't count. But after about twenty to a hundred times the three hundred plus pound bear started to slow down and even stop, sometimes giving me a much needed rest.

Searching for the key that was lost in my pocket somewhere, I opened the truck door a fast as I could but, here comes the bear again and we went around the truck again, and again. When the bear began to slow down, I was able to open the driver's side door while keeping a sharp eye on him but, not having enough time to get in, I shut it quickly and started going around the truck again. After what seemed like forever, I could tell the bear didn't like this game at all, making some sort of grunting sounds, he slowly walked away from the truck disappearing into the dark forest.

Driving down the dark road, heading towards Yosemite to cook freshly caught rainbow trout and spend the night, I started to feel a bit sorry for the bear who was fishing for a trout fisherman. At least he will have a fish story to tell all about on how the trout fisherman got away and I am now convinced, I didn't drink a witches brew, I didn't have a curse put on me from the firepot explosion and as for King George, I can only guess he decided to stop haunting me because more than likely he was betting on the bear to eat the trout fisherman.

ANSWERS TO CHAPTER 6 QUESTIONS

a. Turning around on the trail in a different direction is probably the best option, or not, if that trail ahead is the only way to get to your destination. I don't think flipping a coin is a good option to determine your fate. Waiting a couple hours to give the bear time to move further up or off the trail is another option.

b. You knew you were hiking in bear country, you knew you were going to be around a few bears and you were completely comfortable with that, right? Now that you might meet a bear face to face, are you prepared?

You have purchased all kinds of bear deterrents, read all the bear experts manuals from people who have actually been attacked by bears, more than one air horn, a walking stick for poking the bears eye's out, a whistle to let the bear know your human, a big knife on your belt for whittling wood when bored, and you have stored all of your food in a bear proof container, right? But are you and your little body ready for a violent fight to the death when you encounter a big aggressive three hundred or more pound gladiator bear if it comes to that?

Turning around on the trail in a different direction might still be an option, or who knows, with any luck you might get some good pictures of the peaceful bear grazing in a meadow of daisies.

c. Stepping in a big pile of bear poop might be a fun thing to do at that time but, do your really think it could hide your human scent to an animal that can smell things from two miles away?

CHAPTER 7
WHO SAID FISHING WAS BORING?

("Please don't be mad just because I want to keep all the delicious rainbow trout for myself.")

What would *you* do?
You just come off a trail ending at the trailhead parking lot and see a bear inside your car.

A. Run over to your car and talk to the bear in a calm voice letting him know you do not appreciate the new designer ripped look on the upholstery, but thanks anyways and would he mind posing for a few pictures?

B. Run over to your car, open the door and yell and scream at the top of your lungs for the bear to get out and stop eating your bag of potato chip crumbs!

C. Don't do anything, stay far away from the car and the bear reminding yourself to not leave trash in the car and to vacuum better next time. Hopefully he won't take the car steering wheel with him as a souvenir.

My legs were more than a bit sore after being chased around the truck a hundred times or more by the big bear in the middle of the night. And it was hard for me to believe I was still only on my eight day of the fishing trip, yet here I was once again, sitting in the truck doing more driving after driving all day long.

This vacation was turning into more of a driving road trip then a fishing trip and it was definitely the first time I have been headed towards a Yosemite camp spot with a red as a lobster scabby face, singed off eyebrows, bleeding cracked lips, and the only hair I had left, was on the back of my head!

Not finding any music on the radio to keep me occupied, while the bright head lights maneuver around the dark sharp mountain corners, those oldie but goodie memories started to open again and for some strange reason, I started to remember back to a particular fishing trip I went on in the great state of Oregon. Maybe it had something to do with running through the pitch black forest and all the ghost shadows that were chasing after me along with the bear that made me remember this particular fishing trip. Or maybe, it was the state of Oregon calling me again for another fishing adventure.

Usually, little quirks like these that wander into my mind become the very beginning of how many fishing trips are planned, a wanderlust to be free taking the time to go trout fishing!

And that is exactly what happened a long time ago, back when I was a single man in my early twenties. A little quirk told me to load up the truck and go trout fishing in Oregon!

While I was driving highway five north, through the state of Oregon on a wet and rainy day my truck ran out of gas. Somehow I must have forgotten how far the distances were to each town. This was the first and only time my truck has ever run out of gas.

I had no choice but to try and wave down a passing car hoping some good soul would pick me up and take me to a gas station. After about two hours of standing in the cold rain a white van pulled over, not even thinking of first asking the driver a few questions to make sure he had a normal brain intact, I opened the door and climb in wondering if I was going to make the man mad by getting his seat all wet.

All of a sudden, a smell hit me that was so gross I couldn't help but gage and cough. I was unable to breathe, as if I was taking in some sort of deadly gas from someone who just farted and it immediately reminded me of my buddy Jakes tent!

I looked over to see a smiling big broad shouldered fifty year old guy, with a buzz hair cut and unshaven face, who was getting a kick out of my antics. Gasping for air, I hurriedly rolled down the window sticking my head out into the now drizzling rain.

The van pulled away from the side of the road gaining speed, the driver stretched over his hand, "Billy from Oklahoma. Ran out of gas or the truck break down? Hey, you can keep the window down. It's alright with me. Yeah, the odor is a bit strong if your not use to it."

Seeing his arm reached out from the corner of my eye in a greeting manner, I took in a deep breath holding it, brought my rain splattered head back into the van reached over shaking his hand saying, "I ran out of gas. Forgot how long the distances were here in Oregon."

It was all I could say in that one breathe and quickly moved my head back out to the open window taking in a big gasp of fresh wet air. Thinking the guy probably just let a big fart loose, or maybe one of many, right before I open the door, those kinds of farts could kill a man.

"Well partner, I can get you to a gas station which should be about twenty miles ahead and I have lots of time on my deliveries so I can even give you a ride back."

That was the best news I heard, "Thank you, thank you" I said between the gagging.

For a second, the thought of having Billy stop the van and get out did cross my mind but, I couldn't see myself standing in the rain for hours on end waiting for another good samaritan to pick me up. Although, I wasn't looking forward to sticking my head out the window for the next hour either getting hit by sixty mile an hour rain spatter. I had no choice but to grin and bare it.

Holding in another deep breath, slowly letting it out, I turned towards the big man, "By the way, what are you delivering Billy?" And turn back to the windows fresh air. A person never knows how important fresh air is until they are put into a situation like this one.

With a big grin on his face, he turns the light on in the back of the van, "Turn around and take a look."

I had to ask. Taking in another deep breath, I turn all the way around to see what was in the back of the van. Immediately, now I knew where the smell was coming from. There was a bunk bed metal structure with three beds on each side of the enclosed space, for a total of six beds altogether. The two top bunks were empty, on the four lower beds lay four very white shriveled up people, as if a vampire had suck all the blood out of them. On the top right bunk, lay a banged up middle age man in a dirty suit, that looked like his head had been split in two but there wasn't any blood coming out. Underneath him on the lower bunk, was a very overweight heavy set wrinkled old bald man in farm overalls, with no apparent injury, looking like he was sleeping. On the left upper bunk, was up younger man with half his face missing, wearing what looked like a white t-shirt but was now covered in dried blood that ran down to his blue jeans. And on the last occupied bed, lay an old gray haired lady in a long granny dress, with no apparent injury, wearing a little smile on her face, my guess she was now happy to be in that special place.

One thing that caught my attention was that none of them had any shoes on and each one had a large white tag tied around their big toe.

"Are they dead Billy?" I asked between cough gagging.

Billy was getting such a big kick out of this, he was laughing so hard he could hardly talk, "Of course they are dead but sometimes they sure act like they are alive, sitting up, rolling out of the bunks, moaning and groaning. You're welcome to go back and lie down on the empty bunk if you want."

He wasn't kidding, "No, thanks," I said, between cough attacks. "I'm find just where I am," sticking my head out the window for yet another big gasp of air, feeling every rain drop sting my cold face.

Billy then proceeded to tell me in great detail on how each of the dead people in back came to their particular demise, the guy in the suit, motorcycle accident, no helmet, the young man, car accident, farmer, heart attack, old lady, drug overdose.

Then Billy went on to tell me of all sorts of unbelievable ways people die, afterwards saying it's rare to have anyone just die of old age any more.

It was his job to drive all over the country picking up dead people and delivering them to where the living people wanted them buried.

Billy had a big smile on his face again and I new he just had to tell me something.

"One time I gave a ride to a guy who didn't mind at all sleeping in the back with the lifeless people. What he did when I wasn't looking really pissed me off! I must have stopped for coffee or to use the bathroom, or something. During that time he switched all the tags hanging from the big toes that identified each person and to where they were to be delivered. Well I almost got fired. At the funerals when they opened the caskets they all got a huge surprise. That's not Uncle Paul and he sure didn't change into a little old lady since the last time I saw him!"

Billy's smile disappeared, "If I ever see that guy again, boy is he going to get it!"

Holding in another deep breath of fresh air, I ask him if he ever picked up anyone from a bear attack and he said no, at least not yet.

He also told me that he wished they were in body bags but the company said it was too expensive and the bodies needed to air out or they might get moldy.

"Of course they don't have to smell the dead people for hours on end, driving them around the country like I do!" Billy said.

Billy assured me, that after awhile you get used to the smell, comparing it to road kill. Every now and then, an overly ripe one would come in and make him throw up.

I asked why he wasn't completely freaked out because they were dead people. Wasn't he afraid of ghosts?

Billy gave me a lecture on how the human body was just a shell, just like the shells you collect at the beach. What a person does with the spirit, or soul, while in the shell during their life time makes the difference where they might go afterwards. Think about it, he said.

I was thinking about it and the thought of a bunch of dead people's body's that were just so-called shells washing up on the sea-shore lying all over the beach stinking up the place, before their spirits left than becoming empty shells left me wondering who would ever want to collect those beach shells was not very appealing.

I told Billy I was a trout fisherman and I asked him if he thought I would do any trout fishing after I died because that is what I loved to do most with my shell. Billy assured me more than likely; I would be fishing, because that is what I enjoy the most. Now that was the best news I had heard all day!

Billy went on to say he had all the answers, he was an expert, because while driving around all these dead people spirits started talking asking how this could have happen to them and if somehow he could bring them back to life. He said, I always answer them by saying, "You're talking to the wrong person, I am just the delivery man." And they ask me where they are going and I end up having long conversation with them, mostly listening, to what a person has done while in their shell. I always end up telling them the same thing, "You're talking to the wrong person, I am just the delivery man."

Billy then proceeded to give me some good advice, I swear, I had heard somewhere before. "Don't waste a minute of this precious gift, because before you know it, life could be gone in a flash."

Billy was getting so serious talking about death; I thought I might break his momentum by telling a story that was told to me by some friends.

For some reason, I think it was all the fresh rain air blowing into the back of the van airing out the odor, the potent smell was not bothering me so much. "Hey Billy, I want to tell you a story about what happen to these new parents."

 Billy nodded his head, "Let's hear it!"

"Well, there was these new parents who were pushing their daughter in her stroller at a mall and a very old man who walk with a cane slowly came up to them bending over getting his wrinkled face very close to the little girl, looked her right in the eye saying in a scratchy voice, "Out with the old and in with the new."

Billy was speechless, and didn't say another word, not one. Not one when we stopped at the gas station where I filled up a gas can for the truck or during the whole ride back, not one.

It must have been very thought provoking for him to have a different point of view, which was so simple, when he thought he had all the answers.

Waving goodbye to Billy, who didn't wave back, I was thankful to breathe fresh air again hoping I would not suffer from any long term medical consequences from decomposing corpse gases. And I guess, know it all Billy had some new answer to life's circle of longevity to think about.

After filling the truck up with gas in the drizzling rain, and thank goodness it started right up, it was nice to be on the road again. With a long drive still ahead, I started to think about how I couldn't wait to see my fishing buddies, who lived around the east Salem area, Woodburn, Silverton, and the Mt. Angle area in Oregon. If you have ever been to this part of Oregon then you know how beautiful it is with farms that go on forever. You can smell freshly baked homemade pies and breads in the air, if you're lucky, you can find a place where you can still buy a bottle of un-pasteurized milk with the cream is settling to the top at a country store.

Farm animals dot the rolling green hills filling in the landscape, a picturesque calendar place of red barns and white fences. Long empty pot holed two lane roads go on forever eventually disappearing into the high mountains far in the far distance.

My Oregon buddies Jim and Anthony are always glad to see me because they get to use the same excuse every time to get out of work, telling their employers, "He came all the way here to go fly fishing and it's up to us to show him how good the trout fishing is here in the great state of Oregon!"

With the mention of fishing and the State of Oregon in the same sentence, no employer of Jim or Anthony's would say no to take the day off. After all, the pride of Oregon's good trout fishing reputation was at stake!

One thing that I have learned from my years of fishing with my buddies and the only reason they would let me fish with them again and again is, I had to promise not to tell anyone about the fishing spots they took me to and for that matter, don't tell anyone about the great state of Oregon. It has enough people living in it!

These two trout fishermen know this part of Oregon like the back of their hand and it didn't take long before we were all together on a gray and cold day driving around searching for the perfect fishing spot, turning left here, over the bridge, down the dirt road, up the hill, over another bridge, short cut through a plowed field. I was so turned around before we stopped I could have been in another state and I would not have known it.

We finally pulled over and parked at the only true landmark I would be able to remember, a red covered bridge that was surrounded by a dense wet dripping forest.

While gathering up our fishing gear it was agreed that we would work our way up stream on the left side of the river walking on what was once a dirt road but now a mere muddy trail. The trail itself was a mixture of thorny knee high weeds of tall wet grasses. Jim insisted we start by using his home strung orange and yellow flies with little black tails. I would go first but, only until I caught one, then we would rotate until the dark clouds started raining buckets on us.

We fished all day using wet or dry fly's sending our long lines into the rushing water hour after hour and not one trout among any of us. This was not a little creek but a fast flowing river with nice deep pools swirling along the edge where very large trout usually like to hang out. We all asked ourselves the same question, "How could this river be fished out?" Which anyone, who is a trout fisherman in Oregon, knows is impossible.

Not giving up, following the river through the forest with Jim now way ahead of us Anthony and I, being unmarried at the time, turned our attention to another sport, girls.

Just when I was fishing around to see if he might tell me if he had anyone seriously special, after I told him all about how a true love from high school broke my heart and I would never get over it, we could hear Jim yelling to the top of his lungs and waving his arms.

We started running to see what could be so important?

He kept pointing down in the water saying, "hurry, hurry, look at what's in a river! Look in the river!"

Anthony, who was also a deer hunter couldn't believe what he was seeing, "It's a deer. Who would do such a thing? It could pollute the whole river! What hunter would do that to a deer? Throwing the body parts you don't want into the river and for what? To lighten the heavy load?"

Reaching down into the water, Anthony grabbed a leg by the hoof and pulled the large piece of meat out, "No one used a knife to cut the leg away; it's been completely ripped out by the joint. Just look at the skin and tendons here. Who would have the strength to do that? Something tore the legs completely off the animal and threw them in the river and took the rest. Man, look at the claw gashes that have been dug into that hide!"

Wondering what my fishing buddies had gotten me into, I asked, "Should we be looking out for something that might tear our limbs off? A lion, a bear?"

I don't know if Jim was just trying to scare me or was telling the truth but I have known Jim to be always forthcoming and truthful, "Well Danny McGee, I guess we never told you about the Sasquatch sightings around here. I didn't believe it myself, until I actually saw one and I'm not the only one who saw it.

Anthony was busy trying to get the rest of the legs with a hook from his fishing pole, carefully balancing on the edge of the river, trying hard not to fall in and get wet saying, "Yah, I believe what people say is completely true and now, here's proof!"

All right, these guys were starting to scare me just a little, and I reminded myself of why I came, "Let's get back to trout fishing!"

Like a magic word, Jim and Anthony stopped looking down at the deer legs in the water, following right behind me. I could hear Jim say to Anthony, "We'll pick them up on the way back."

We didn't get very far fishing before we came across an old weather beaten Victorian house, a small ways from the river in a large clearing surrounded by a thick wooded forest. At one time, it was a well kept up house, but by the look of the overgrown rose garden; it was easy to see no one had lived here for at least five years.

The other fishermen, and I, agreed right away it would be a great place to live, a trout river right out your front door and not a noisy neighbor in sight!

The house itself was in good shape, not a broken window or a budging shiplap board. It just needed a fresh coat of white paint.

We peered through the windows from the large front porch, trying to get a better view of what the house looked like on the inside. From what we could see, the rooms had a fresh coat of light green paint on the ceilings, and had a floral print wallpaper going up to the crown molding. I could not see one piece of furniture anywhere.

Curiosity told Anthony to try the beveled glass front door, which opened easily and he motioned us to follow inside. Leaning our fishing poles on the outside wall, Jim and I followed Anthony around the house, inspecting every room. It was a very nice house, clean as a whistle, and even the kitchen floors were spotless.

Why then was no one living here, I had to ask myself? A light bulb went off in my head, the attic! Running back to the hallway, I stood looking up at the cover to the entrance, hurriedly waving Jim over, "Come on and give me a boost up, maybe they left behind something valuable."

Jim put his hands together, making a stirrup, sending me up so fast, I barely had time to put my hands up before hitting the cover, sending it flying somewhere into the attic.. Using all the arm strength I had, I lifted myself up into a dimly lit room. The only light came from a small bevel octagon shaped glass window set at end of the low pitched gable roof.

"Hey, there are some old Victorian lady's shoes up here. They got pointed toes and lots of laces. Want me to throw them down?"

Since I did not hear a clear reply, just some vague stomping and running sounds, intermixed with grunting noises, I went on to the next prize, a box of newspapers. I could not believe my eyes, 1921 was the date, probably corresponded to the time the first people lived in the house.

Rummaging through the papers, I kept hearing some strange sort of mumbling, almost a growling, like from a mean dog giving a warning before he bites, coming from the attic access opening.

Thinking the guys are just fooling around, "Hey, wait until you see these old newspapers, I'll throw some down."

Grabbing a big handful, standing up careful not to bump my head, curiosity told me to check out the view from the small attic window. As I moved closer, I could not believe what I was seeing through the glass! There in front of me, down on the overgrown lawn in the backyard, I could see Jim and Anthony running as fast as they could out from behind the house!

Now, if my fishing buddies are running in the back yard, then who was I talking to down below in the hallway? Getting more than just a little scared, I moved over to the crawl hole, trying to get a look at what ever was down there. "Hey, you guys still down there?"

The answer came back in a shallow voice like someone trying to talk to you with food in their mouth.

Now I was really scared. Was some unearthly thing telling me to come down so he could rip my limbs off my body?

I was scared to death! I was trapped! Running back to the little window I could see my buddies waving for me to get out. My face must have looked as white as a ghost! I thought of busting out the window and climbing out, but the window was way too small. There was no way I could squeeze through. The only way out, was the way I came in, down the attic access hole right into the jaws of the monster waiting for me. The same monster that got the deer and I really didn't want my legs and arms ripped away from my body. Anxiety was setting in.

"What to do, what to do?"

I had better do something, or that monster could be climbing up through the hole any second, and all I had was a bunch of newspapers and pair of old lady's shoe's to defend myself, "Oh… what to do, what to do?"

Is this how my life will end? A trout fisherman ripped apart and eaten by Bigfoot! Eventually ending up as monster poop? Not if I can help it!

I conjured up all the strength my mind and body had, realizing the fact that the attic hole was the only way in and out. Trying my hardest to get even a glimpse of what might be waiting to eat me, I looked down the hole, only seeing the hallway wood floor.

Taking in a deep breath, I threw the bundle of newspapers I held in my arms down the hole, I wanted to see if it would attack them. If it did, I could jump on its back maybe stunning the thing and get away.

I looked and listen, nothing.

With one last deep breath, thinking it just might be my last breath, I jumped down the hole hitting the floor hard falling over from the long drop. I was up fast! The fear adrenalin sent my legs running faster than they have ever run before, without taking one look behind me, I ran down the hallway into the kitchen, and seeing the back door was already open, made me think I just might have a chance. Only a wooden screen door blocked the way, and I knew most screen doors open out. I put both my hands straight out in front to me and smashed right into it, sending the door crashing against the back of the house, "Bam!!" I ran barreling out onto the lawn not stopping until I ran around the house and up the river to where my buddies were standing.

Bent over and gasping for air, I asked, "Did you see it?"

Jim and Anthony looked at me like I was crazy, "Of course we saw that huge hairy thing and I've never seen anything so ugly! What? You didn't you see it?"

I could barley catch my breath. "Hey, after I saw you two running from the house, and that thing was talking gibberish to me; I wasn't going to stick around to see who, or what it was. I have never been so scared in my whole life!"

Jim standing with his hands in his jeans pockets looking a bit shaken, "Dang, we saw Sasquatch again and don't have a camera just like the last time. How is anyone ever going to believe us without proof!

"You got that right" says Anthony, "Now who's going back for the fishing poles?"

At least I was honest, "I don't think getting my arm and a leg pulled out of my body is worth a fishing pole. Although, that pole sure has a lot of memories, I really hate to lose it."

With the truth out, Anthony and Jim agreed it wouldn't be worth getting all dead over a fishing pole. Jim shrugged his shoulders in complete disappointment, turning towards downstream and starting walking.

Jim taking a long deep breath, "The first thing I am going to do when I get back is buy a camera!

On our long walk back to the car, along the river where nobody even wanted to look at the mauled deer parts, Anthony was doing his best to keep the adrenaline going, "Hey, I could take you guys to a place tonight where a half human, half dog with antlers lives in the woods and only comes out at night. I've seen it! The thing stands six feet tall, has a hairless head with four point antlers on it, short pointed ears and a long hairy body, hands and feet like a person. You drive to this one spot in the woods, bring food like a steak, or hamburger, park, and put the food on the hood of the car, turn off your lights and wait quietly. Within an hour, you see this thing come out of the woods and start munching on the steak. You turn the lights on, which completely freaks the thing out and it starts attacking the car. It's scary as hell. Want to go?"

Shaking my head in disbelief, "No one was going to believe what just happen to us, let's just keep this to us."

Anthony had other ideas. "You have to be kidding. I'm not going to keep quite. I'm going to tell everyone I meet; I'm going to offer ten bucks to anyone to retrieves my fishing pole, and when I get yours back, I'll sell them back to you guys!"

On the long rainy ride bac, slipping and sliding over bumpy newly plowed muddy fields, I started to think about how going trout fishing is not just about catching fish, sometimes it's about experiencing an unforgettable adventure that will scare the pants right off you.

Remembering those old good times with my Oregon friends is always fun as I went back to concentrating on staring out at the headlights lighting up the dark road lined with tall black sticks of pine trees listening to the hum of the engine, but I just couldn't resisted pulling a big itching scab off my forehead. The long drive was starting to take its toll on my sleepy brain. I started to wish someone would invent a small coffee maker to plug into the outlet on my truck dashboard. A hot cup a coffee would be perfect right now on my long drive to a Yosemite Valley Campground.

ANSWERS TO CHAPTER 7 QUESTIONS

a. I have actually stood next to some people who had a bear in their car and it was the cutest thing they had ever seen saying, "Oh honey, doesn't he look just like a big cuddly teddy bear? Here take the camera and take a picture as close as you can. No one back home will believe we actually had a bear in our car!"

After the bear left the car, the people's attitude change completely, "That bear didn't have to break the window! Look, the door doesn't even shut right. How much is that going to cost to fix. And look at all the rips in the front and back seats, and that smell; I'm not driving all the way home with that smell! Did he leave one of his you know what's? Now who's going to clean that up? The car's junk. It's going to be in the shop forever and I bet they will never get that smell out!"

b. If you have never seen an angry bear, get ready, because you are about to experience one. How much do you weigh? How many canine teeth do you have, and how many sharp claws on your paws?

c. This is the no brainier answer. After all, not much you can do, but watch and stay far away. Hopefully when the bear is finished, he doesn't smell the granola energy bar in your day pack hanging from your shoulder.

CHAPTER 8
ONE TROUT FISHERMAN SUNNY SIDE UP PLEASE

("Bear, what bear, I don't see a bear, let's get fishing!")

What would *you* do?

You're sitting in lawn chair fishing at a beautiful Alpine Lake, when a black bear comes out of the woods and walks right in front of you, backs up sticking his big smelly hairy butt in front of your face while you watch the bear get busy pulling your stringer line out of the water with the three nice rainbow trout hooked onto it.

A. Jump up, and run away as fast as you can, because the bear might eat you next! After all, you are a trout fisherman and to a hungry bear trout fisherman probably taste like trout.

B. Stay seated, talk to the big bear in a calm voice asking him nicely to quit eating your fish and could he please get his left over dried poop matted butt out of your face?

C. Get up and hit the bear with your fishing poll than throw your lawn chair at him yelling, "Turn around you will have to fight for my fish!"

Slowing the truck way down, after seeing a yellow sign of another approaching sharp corner on the dark mountain road, I found myself completely side tracked dreaming of a hot cup of coffee. Reaching around on the seat for some lemon drops, thinking that might side track me from pulling scabs off my chin, my hand found the fish bag full of Merced River trout. I was is such a hurry to get away from that bear, that chased me around the truck, I forgot all about stopping to put them in the ice chest.

Pulling the truck over at the first turnout I came to, I grabbed the fish bag and made a quick dash on my sore wobbly legs to the back of the truck. Opening the camper shell as fast as I could, I put the fish safely in the cold ice chest and for a second, I thought for sure I heard something rustling in the woods. Was anywhere safe?

Maybe it was time to sell the truck and buy a van and then I would not be out here in the dark feeling bear eyes stalking me.

Closing the camper shell door I crossed my fingers, knowing I could not play another game of, "Run around the truck bear gets to try and eat a trout fisherman," again. My legs felt like rubber, my sleepy head felt like the planet mars ready to pop from the exploding fire pit and I just had to pull another itching scab off my forehead. I was not feeling so good.

Getting back on the road wanting to lift my spirits, I started to think of how I should cook the trout I caught today. I really didn't have time to start a fire and smoke one next to the fire pit. That meant the gas cook stove was my only choice, filet one cooking it in butter with a dash of tarragon, dill, salt, pepper and a squirt of lime, yummy. Maybe a side of canned chili to go with it, I was starved! I could taste it already!

No wonder I was getting grouchy, my stomach was growling for food and continued to growl the whole time until I reached one of my favorite campgrounds in Yosemite Valley, Upper Pines.

It must have been around 10pm by the time I pulled into a campsite and I was surprised how empty the whole campground was even for a week day. Getting out of the truck stretching my stiff leg muscles, I could tell the air had a definite chill of frost sending my every breath into a white cloud. The chill even started to bring the temperature of my red face way down. I was feeling better, maybe my luck had changed, "trout fisherman out smarted a big black bear running around the truck," that is funny, giving myself a pat on the back.

This time of year is one of the best times to go camping in Yosemite because not many people want to brave the spring mountain snow storms and the cold winds, giving me the opportunity to pick out a perfect campsite.

Turning on a bright lantern, setting it on the picnic table, gave off plenty of light to move everything I needed out from the truck. Not forgetting I was in bear country, I put two ice chests and a dry food crate in the bear locker right away, taking out only one fish and a can of chili. If the bears did come, I thought, at least they would not get much to eat, because I would be devouring this meal in a matter of seconds!

Moving as fast as my frozen fingers could go, I filet the big trout just like I had planned and carefully laid it down into a hot sizzling pan next to my can of bubbling chili sitting on top of the other hot burner.

When a growling stomach hollers for food sometimes the food just can't cook fast enough and with a little sample bite here, carefully maneuvering the spoon past my scabby lips, a little sample there, all of a sudden the meal has been completely eaten before it even had a chance to get to a plate! "Mmn…Mmn…," It was so good my only regret was that I didn't cook two trout.

After cleaning the frying pan, throwing the trash away, going to the restroom, brushing my teeth, washing my face, and doing whatever chores needed to be done, I wanted to sit back in my camper shell and relax. Looking around the dark campsite I thought that I had forgotten something but couldn't quite figure out what it was. "Oh well, the important thing is everything is locked up tight in the bear locker, nothing is left in the cab of my truck that will give a bear a reason to break in." I assured myself.

It must have been close to 12:30pm when I finally took the lantern, open the back of the camper shell door by turning the handle sending the door up automatically in a speedy swish. Climbing in over the tailgate into the inside of the camper shell, reached up, pulled the door down by its silver handle closing it. I then turned the handle to the right, which slides two horizontal poles outward securing the door against the inner frame.

The inside of camper shell is small, because of the height of the ceiling, you are only able to kneel while moving around or you will hit your head, which hurts like the dickens. It's not unusual for me to be walking around with a few lumps the size of a half egg on my head while camping, one reason why I tent when I can. At least the ceiling in a tent is a bit softer.

Snuggled up in my sleeping bag, I new it was way too late to get any kind of reading in, so I just laid back, looking around under the glow of the lantern light, surveying my most precious and prized possessions. Fly rod, spinning rod, tackle box, rubber boots, hiking boots, car chains, rain gear, camera, book, a backpack of clothes, my precious fishing treasure map rolled up in the p.v.c. tube, fishing vest with hooks flies and who knows what else in the pockets, "maybe that should have been in the bear locker, nah, its late and I am to tired to do that now." And once again, looking over to the inside of the camper shell door, I notice the missing lock.

I guess it's all about priorities. I never miss the inside lock on the camper shell door until at a time like this, when I'm ready to go to sleep. I've always thought it would be nice to have a lock on the inside of the camper shell door, to keep any potential burglars from opening it from the outside and terrorizing me while I was asleep. Of course you can lock the camper shell door handle with a key from the outside, but once you're on the inside of the camper shell, the door is always unlocked. There is only a small silver handle and if you turn it to the left, it pulls two small horizontal poles inward; activating the air shock hinges which automatically lifts the door open straight up in a speedy swish. Then you can either open the tail gate with its handle, or just climb over the tail gate to get in or out of the camper shell.

Since I've never had a problem with anyone breaking into my truck, I told myself once again not to worry about it. Instead I tried to concentrate on the beautiful day of trout fishing I just had and how my luck had changed. With a belly full of fresh trout, the cool air massaging my red beet face, my legs tired from acting like a bull dozer crashing through the woods and playing ring around the rosy, run around the truck game with a bear at night, I was going to sleep like a log. With that thought, I crawled deep into my sleeping bag, moved my rough sand paper lips back and forth, wondering if I should pull off another piece of charcoal crispy skin, decided not to, because I didn't want my sleeping bag to get bloody, leaned over and turned out the lantern, closing my eyes to a peaceful nights sleep.

My eyes were not closed very long, something was not right, I started to hear small cracking noises out in the night forest moving around. I heard it again. The sound of small twigs breaking under a heavy weight was getting closer. It was way too big for a coyote, raccoon, or a fox. Maybe someone was coming down from backpacking in the high country? Or it could be one of those clueless hikers, who, stunned by the beauty of Yosemite National Park kept going and going, never realizing darkness falls quick in the mountains and that it's a long, very long, hike back to camp especially without a flashlight! I should talk after my little excursion through the dark forest today.

Trying to rationalize what could be making the noise, all the while knowing perfectly well who it was, and I new it couldn't be hiker because it was moving way too slowly. Maybe someone was sneaking around like a thief? What are they going to do? Break into my truck for a few coins? Maybe there looking for a fancy car stereo? Or, it could be the Ranger? I don't think Park Rangers ever sleep.

I could hear loud breathing, sniffing along the side of the truck. Now the hair on the back of my neck started to stand straight up, wondering what my big friend was up to. Yep, I new exactly who that big nose belong to and now his big nose was sniffing right on the outside of my trucks camper shells back door! The very and only place to get in or out!

I sat up trying to get a better look out the dark tinted windows, I couldn't see a thing, only hear the grunting and sniffing coming from something by the camper shell back door, than, "Bam!"

"What the…." The bear was trying to get into the back of the camper shell by smashing the plastic window in!

"Bam!"

The bear hit the window again and in bringing his paw down from the swing hit the outside door handle! Right before my eyes in a split second flash, I watch to see the silver handle turn half way!

The bear hit the camper window again, "Bam!"

The handle turned even more! I quickly tried to reach out and grab from the inside to prevent it from turning anymore, but I was too late! The camper shell door flung right open in a big swish and there in front of me was a huge head of a big mean wild black bear! His mouth was wide open, showing a full set of white shinny canine razor sharp teeth! Apparently not happy to see me at all!

"Rrrr…arr…grr!"

It grunted and snorted as it reached out two big paws gripping onto the tail gate pushing his big hairy head right in to the small space, coming right at me, he was coming in!

"Rrrr…arr…grr!"

I had absolutely no where to go! Smashing myself against the back of the camper shell scared out of my wits! I had only a split second before the drooling man eating bear with huge teeth would start taking big chunks out of my body! I reached for the closest thing available, my lucky fishing pole, but the bear was standing on it!

"Yikes! I was one dead trout fisherman for sure!"

The wild bear could take off half my face with one swipe of his paw, I was a dead man and 300 hundred pounds of bear was now more than half way in my camper shell with chopping fangs less the two feet away from my face! Panicking franticly I reach around for anything I could get my hands on. All I could do was stare right into the beast two fierce black eyes on that huge hairy head, and watch like in a slow motion movie his drooling chomping fangs coming closer and closer! I had my hand on something, my camera! Fumbling, I quickly grabbed it with two hands holding straight out in front of me pushing the button, "Click," sending a bright flash right into the eyes of the bear!

"Aaarr…ffff…aaarr!" The bear shook his head back and forth. "Oerrr…arr!, Oerr…arr!"

It let out a pain roar so loud I hurried to put my hands over my ears! I was just waiting for the impact of a swipe to hit my head at any second. I reached out and flashed the camera again, "click," the flash went off sending the bear into another ear shrieking roar. This time the bear started backing up so I flashed the camera again and again, backing up the huge bear further and further, until he was completely out of the camper shell!

My heart was pounding right out of my skin! I held the camera in front of me moving quickly to open door, sticking my head out to make sure the bear was gone.

"Yep, he's gone alright, and right now he is a very angry bear!"

Reaching up, I grabbed the door handle and pulled it down until it closed, twisting the handle checking to make sure the horizontal poles were secure against the inside wall. Once again I reminded myself to, fix that lock!!!

Taking a deep breath, I was shaking so bad I didn't know what to do next. Turning on the lantern, I looked down at all the bear slobber on my sleeping bag, everything happened so fast! I was so lucky! I couldn't believe that the batteries hadn't gone out in the camera like they usually do. That camera has never work right from day one, it's been dropped, lost in snow, sank in mud, I even wondered why I kept it around.

Then for some reason, I started laughing, it was funny, how I keep finding myself in these death defying circumstances with bears, yet I always seem to find a way to get away. So, having nothing better to do at the moment, I made up little song to a nursery rhyme melody of, "Hush little baby, don't say a word, mamas going to…"

It went like this,

"One big bear comes along,
 Wants to eat a trout fisherman all day long,

Another big bear wants some too,
Little does he know the trout fisherman to fast for you,

A big bear smells a treat,
And wants a trout fisherman that's good to eat,

That big bear will have wait,
To see if he can get passed the tailgate,

Little does he know what is waiting for him,
He better smile for a trout fisherman

Reality sets in as I realize I am trapped in the camper shell and the nights not over yet. How lucky can one person be not getting eaten by two bears in one day?

I started to focus on what the big bear will do when he recovers from his blindness? I guess that will depend on how hungry he is and if he does come back, will the camera batteries hold out? Or, what if another bear, two or even five bears try to get into the camper shell? How could I sleep with the fear of a bear breaking in at any moment? But to leave, I would have to open the door to the camper shell, crawl over the tail gate and head for the driver's seat. Somehow then I would have to get to the bear locker retrieving my ice chest, food box and stuff them into the back of the truck. Would the bear be

153

waiting in the black of the night for pay back and a midnight snack on the side?

As to why the bear decided to climb into the camper shell was not a complete mystery, even though I didn't keep any food in my camper shell. The bear must have smelled the scent of a trout on my fishing vest, or could he have smelled the trout scent on my stringer line sitting inside my tackle box. Or, a few trout scales on my boots from cleaning them, giving the bear the idea that a few nice fresh rainbow trout might be waiting for him inside the camper shell. Maybe it was the trout scent on my hands from filleting the trout tonight, even though I wash them with soap and water afterwards. I would bet any money the bear just couldn't resist my good cooking and was attracted to the smell of nicely cooked trout scent all over me!

Once that bear opened the camper shell door, and not seeing so well in the dark, he probably saw and smelled, the biggest flip flopping well cooked trout he had ever seen. In reality, what he found was a sunny side up trout fisherman having a wild surprise party!

What was that noise? Did I hear bear foot steps again? What's that? Was it another bear sniffing around the truck? Or was it the same bear determined to get some trout? Maybe it's the truck! I bet the whole truck smells like trout and it's attracting every black bear in Yosemite! Maybe the truck smells so much like a trout to a bear; it even looks like one enormous trout!

Right then I knew I had to make a break for it or I would have a hungry bear on top of me again before the night was over. I only had so much ammo left in the camera and I decided to use it to get away.

I had to let this bear know I was in here and for him to stay away. My lantern was already on and that didn't seem to make a difference. Taking the end of my fishing pole I started hitting everything in the camper shell to make as much noise as possible. Then I stopped and listened. I made some more noise, and listened again.

Did the bear care if I was making all this noise? The only way to really tell was to make a break for it and try to escape from the bear infested campground.

Putting on my pants and boots I had to act fast. I was determined to get into the bear locker, where the real smorgasbord was, grab the ice chest filled with all my camping goodies which included the fresh trout and run back to the truck before the bears intercept me. Run back again to the food locker grab the other food box filled with can goods and bring it back the truck speeding away. On second thought, if I put both the ice chest and the food box on the front seat of the truck then I wouldn't have to go all the way around to the back each time making the escape even faster.

The time had come, with the camera in one hand, car keys and lantern in the other ready as I will ever be, I slowly turned the door handle. Slowly pushing the camper shell door open, I steady my arm holding the camera in front of me looking both ways into the cold darkness waiting to be attacked any second. I could see absolutely nothing in the black of night, except the light from the lantern glowing off the ground and trees. I knew darn well more than one wild bear was out there and I new my every move was going to be watched. Whatever moon was out earlier must have gone on the other side of the mountain, which made this task even harder.

My heart was pounding a thousand beats a second as I moved one leg over the tail gate than the other. I stood waiting to be blind sided, torn apart to smithereens, nothing, in a split second dash I ran a fast as I could around to the front of the truck fumbling with my keys to get in.

"Come on, come on," finally getting the key into the slot, "Click."

Pulling up the door handle swinging the door wide open, I smash my head against the top frame trying to get in quickly sitting down slamming the door behind me.

"Whew!" I made it.

My hyperventilating deep breaths started to immediately fog up the window, I was shaking like a leaf scared out of my skin and for a second even thought of leaving everything in the bear locker, just start driving. I compared the odds, one dead trout fisherman eaten by bears, or one very hungry sad but alive trout fisherman. I had made up my mind.

The truck started right up, "varrrummm."

Revving the engine was a sound bears did not like, turning on the bright headlights should be another deterrent, I kept telling myself.

Clinching my teeth, with the camera strung around my neck, I leaned over unlocking the passenger side door. The head lights gave off just enough light to see where the food locker was at the campsite. Making a quick dash out of the driver's side door around the front of the truck I ran to the food locker pulled its lock to the side swung the door open reaching in grabbing an ice chest. I ran as if a bear was chasing me back to passenger side of the truck pulling the door handle open balancing the ice chest on my knee than setting it on the floor. I ran back again to the food locker, grabbing the heavy food box, reminding myself not bring so many cans next time and ran back to the truck setting it on the seat. Back one more time for the last ice chest, setting it on the food box slamming the door. In a split second flat, I ran around to the front of the truck and jump right into the driver's seat shutting the door behind me, "Whew, I made it!"

Taking deep breaths telling myself what I just did was completely nuts because I could have been eaten by a Jurassic animal at any time, I put the truck in gear and started to slowly pull onto the asphalt road.

Still something was not quite right. The truck did not handle in its usual way, it felt like a lot of extra weight was in the truck camper shell bed, as if I was carrying a load of bricks. Then I remembered that I had forgotten to shut the back camper shell door when I climbed out.

Slamming on the breaks I felt the whole truck heave forward as if a big weight just shifted or I should say rolled all the way to the front of the camper shell in a big loud solid thug sound, "bam!"

"Uh, oh," I thought to myself, "I don't think the bear liked that very much."

With a big shift of bear weight, the truck bed leaned to the left, than with an unbalanced rock of the truck back and forth, than a solid lean to the right, the heavy weight was completely lifted off the truck.

Looking in my rear view mirror into the glow of the red brake lights I could make out the outline of one very big stumbling bear. Putting the pedal to the medal I sped out of that campground before another bear decided to go for a ride.

Here I was, after driving most of the day and now I'm driving again in the middle of the night a trout fisherman running away from the hungry bears. Was anywhere safe? And it's still only the eight day of my fishing trip!!!

ANSWERS TO CHAPTER 8 QUESTIONS

a. Good idea and just hope the bear is so concentrated on eating your fish he won't chase you and eat you next! What other options do you have?

b. Get ready, because the bear will definitely be looking at you for food next and I don't think the bear understands the English language.

c. Do you feel lucky? Toss a coin, might work to scare the bear away but, what if it doesn't? Then what do you plan do with a wounded three hundred pound angry bear confronting you?

CHAPTER 9
EASY PICKENS

*("You think I have trout is this bag and you
want to take a look?")*

It was a very, very, long night finally making a decision
to drive to my next destination in the southeastern part of
Yosemite national park, Tuolumne Meadows. The
adrenalin from my encounter with the black bear
drooling on top of me in the back of the camper shell
kept my eyes wide open hour after hour. The only other

thing keeping me busy was picking my scabby lip, watching brightly lit up road signs as they whizzed by and trying to spot any nocturnal animals getting ready to cross the road. I didn't see a one, not even my friend the wild bear, who is not necessarily a nocturnal animal when it comes to searching for easy pickens food.

When it comes to food, bears are out all times of the day trying to fatten up.

Pulling into the first campsite I came upon at Tuolumne Meadows campground sometime in the early a.m. I had a definite agenda. To clear everything out from the back of my truck that might have even have the slightest fish scent on it and stuff it into the campsite's bear locker.

The camper shell door was still wide open, looking inside with the lantern shaking my head I could see the bear had made one big mess tearing up my stuff, "This is going to take forever!"

It wasn't long before I found out that it would be impossible to fit everything with a fish scent on it into the bear locker, unless it was the whole truck complete with all of its contents including me!

The only thing that would fit in the small bear locker were the one ice chest containing my most prized possession and the crate of cans, the rest was up to chance.

Doing the nightly chores was a real pain, literally, trying to wash a scabby face without bleeding was just impossible, even opening my mouth to brush my teeth scabs would crack with small bits landing on my tooth brush.

I was crawling over the tail gate into the back of the camper shell, staring down at my now newly ripped apart bear slobbery sleeping bag, I wondered if I was going to get any sleep at all tonight. Reaching up once again, grabbing hold of the handle to the camper shell door slowly pulling it down I notice the missing lock, "Please, not another bear tonight," I pleaded.

Now I could go sleep in the truck cab and let the bears have a wildlife party in the camper shell but then I put the equation together. Three hundred pound bear dancing around like a maniac verses a thin wall camper shell. The camper shell would lose and I would be without shelter. The only thing to do was protect my property!

With camera by my side I lay down and closed my eyes still feeling the fire pit explosion on my throbbing face, especially my cheeks. Trying not to think of all my aches and pains I listened to the light mountain breeze tickling the pine trees. I started to think that maybe, just maybe, not only did the truck have a permanent trout scent but I was also carrying a permanent trout scent. My boots definitely have a few fish scales left on them, my clothes have a fish scent on them from cleaning the fish, even my breath smells like fish from eating so many and the smoke trout scent is permanently in my stubble hair. Had I become a walking cooked fish dinner for wild bears? As if someone was shouting out, "One sauté trout fisherman for any hungry bear who wants one!"

And with me camping in the truck, of course the inside of the truck would have a trout scent to attract the bears. What was I thinking? No wonder the bears have been after me.

I was up all night tossing and turning just waiting for a big bear to come and eat me. Right at dawn, as soon as the first morning light peaked through the trees, I was out of bed and I had a plan for my ninth day of vacation. After breakfast I would wash clothes, clean boots, go shower, brushed my teeth extra good hopefully not breaking to many scabs and wiped down everything with soap, including the truck inside and out, anything that might have a trout scent on it. At the visitor center I would pick up more batteries for the camera, a travel pad lock to try and lock the inside of the camper shell door, buy a few new pots, and pans to bang on, (I didn't want to dent my good one's,) a whistle, air horn and if any bear tried to get into the back of my camper shell again he was in for an even bigger surprise party!

That little project took all morning and I finally gave up, because it became utterly impossible to get the trout scent off everything. I came to the conclusion that I would have to defend myself again if necessary.

For the rest of day nine, I hiked over polished granite domes, up to a waterfall and even took a nice nap in a grassy meadow next to a babbling brook. The brook was babbling so loud I really thought I would have to find a new spot but I didn't move. Actually I think it's monotonous, "Babble, babble, babble, go fishing, babble, babble, babble go fishing," put me right into a deep sleep waking up to only thoughts of going fishing.

I have often hiked with people who say, "If you listen hard, you will hear the babbling brook telling you the meaning of life."

A hard as I have tried, all I have ever been able to hear is, "Babble, babble, babble, go fishing. Babble, babble, go fishing." That was good news, the meaning of life, for me, was to go fishing!

Back at camp, I was reluctant to have my favorite meal for dinner of rainbow trout but then again, I decided I wasn't going to let a few bears stop me. My dinner menu consisted of a nice fourteen inch fish with a few drips of lemon on the inside, adding butter, a dash of basil, paprika and a few sliced almonds. Wrapping it in tinfoil, I laid it on the fire ring grill next to a large potato, and a can of green beans. Banana cream pudding was for desert, "yummy."

Was I afraid of another exploding fire pit? Sure I was, and came up with a solution. I found a nice bendable stick, tying a string around the top end and the bottom end making a bow, and of course I made a small arrow. My plan was to set the tip of the arrow on fire and shoot it into the fire pit where my kindling was neatly stacked up.

Right when I was about to light the end, I started to think of, "what if" some kid saw me shooting a flaming arrow into the fire pit, or the ranger. Thinking this was not such a good idea, I instead, tied a bunch of short sticks together to make one long one. Then I wrapped the end with a piece of paper, lighting it, and slowly pushed it toward the fire ring into the kindling. In a matter of seconds I had a nice safe camp fire started. Believe me; I never ever want to experience a small nuke explosion again!

While enjoying my scrumptious dinner, carefully missing my burnt lips with every bite, I couldn't help to think of what my friend, who came for a nice visit in my camper shell to have his picture taken, was having for dinner. A few nuts with berries, young grasses on the side, and for dessert a big black stink bug! Or, he's nonchalantly walking threw a campground scaring off all the campers who run away in a panic leaving behind all the tasty treats. By now, I am sure there were not any long lasting effects from the flash camera and has now forgotten all about the trout fisherman he almost had for dinner the night before.

When dinner was over, I thought it was a perfect time to go trout fishing, after all the babbling brook told me that was the meaning of life, a trout fisherman's life.

Whether I fished up stream or down stream, using rooster tail spinners, I had an eerie creepy feeling a bears eyes were watching me and I was constantly looking over my shoulder. Look left, "What was that sound in the bushes." Look right, "what was that sound." I was ready for a big bear to jump out of the bushes and start chewing on my trout smelling leg at any second.

Giving up on the trout fishing idea, even though the babbling brook told me that was the meaning of life but kind of left out that it might also be the end of my life because I could feel those teeth that I saw last night chewing on one of my body parts, I thought it might be best to travel out of Yosemite bear country.

Back at camp, I open the fisherman's treasure map on the picnic table, "Yep, some nice relaxing trout fishing was just what I needed, without a bunch of bears watching me."

Looking down at the town of Lee Vinning, Mono Lake, the road up to Bridgeport and down to the June Lake Loop, Lake Crawly, Tom's Place, Bishop, Owens River,

Mammoth Lakes, on the eastern side of the California High Sierras Mountain Range, was all the encouragement I needed. It would all depend on if Tioga pass was open at 9945 feet in elevation. I brought snow chains and should have nothing to worry about, it's been a very dry winter and no big snow storms were in the forecast.

The eastern side of the Sierras is a trout fisherman's paradise. There are more secret fishing spots hidden here than you could shake a stick at. From the big brown trophy trout, to alpine rainbows, golden and cut throats are here among the most beautiful scenery of towering snow capped mountain peaks, surrounded by lakes and rivers in pine forests. And of course, I am not the only hungry creature that enjoys this delicacy of fesh mountain fish raccoons, foxes, baggers, eagles, ospreys, and my scary friends the black bears.

Having so many choices to fish for, I decided to retire to my bed in the camper shell pick a few more scabs off my bleeding cheek and try to make up my mind where to fish. I also came to the conclusion that I have known since becoming a trout fisherman no matter where I go fishing the bears have always want to eat a trout fisherman.

That night was restless and sleepless as usual, I was listening to every little noise in the woods just staring at the silver handle waiting for a bear to turn it sending the door opening a speedy swish. I was unable to get a lock for it. Although, I was prepared, the visitor center had some bear deterrents and I bought plenty of batteries for the camera. Who could sleep? Knowing a hungry people eating bear might be upon me at any moment ripping me to shreds.

Finally morning, a bright orange glow of sunrise shined through the camper shell window on day ten, giving me just enough light to get up and start moving around.

I started to chuckle, remembering how unprepared I was for any kind of bear attack and now that I was prepared, nothing happens. I was taught a good lesson I will never forget, be prepared for a bear encounter at anytime in bear country. Because if you're not prepared when a hungry bear shows up, and he's not finding anything to his liking except you, then you have a big problem on how to stay alive. All bears are completely unpredictable.

After a couple trout, eggs, with toast, breaking open only a few scabs open on my lip from the sandpaper crispiness of the bread, I was off driving east and crossing my fingers Tioga Pass would be open. If it was, I would soon be at one of my favorite fishing spots in the June Lake Loop, hoping the trout named King George was still waiting for me.

I would not even mind seeing my nice bear friend again, from the last time I stayed at June Lake, with the big sniffing nose right outside my tent. He really was a nice bear.

Why was he such a nice bear? And why did he stay all night on the outside my tent? All I could think of is that trout fisherman smell fishy and some bears like smelling trout fisherman but not eating them. That is my only guess as to why a big silly bear sat outside of my tent all night long pushing his nose against the thin material taking in enormous sniffing whiffs.

This bear did not want to eat me, I could tell by his mannerism, he wasn't grunting aggressively, moving his head back and forth, or trying to get into my tent. He just wasn't the, "I'm going to eat you," kind of bear. I think he was full of food and just like the scent of a trout fisherman. For two nights I didn't get any sleep just because this bear decided make himself comfortable and nap right against my tent. Every now and then he would push his big nose against the thin material taking in big sniffs making a few slurpee sounds.

At first, I was scared out of my wits being woken up at eleven at night by a sniffing bear pushing his big nose against my tent thinking he was going to eat me. I lay perfectly still not moving a muscle, trying to make the bear think I was fast asleep. It must have worked because all the bear did until sunrise, besides walk around the tent a few times, was sit on his behind and sniff the air.

"What a wonderful smell," the bear must have thought, "fresh trout fisherman!"

Finally, on the third night I went and slept in the truck, because I really wanted to get a good night sleep and I was a bit worried the bear might change his mind and eat a fresh trout fisherman.

In the morning, only one set of bear paw prints were next to the tent. The bear must have been very sad not to get his nightly fish sniffs and I felt a bit sorry for him, after all, he was minding his manners.

Driving through the green meadows of the high country, past pristine cobalt blue lakes, the green forest ends at timberline on the glacier mountain. Patches of pure white snow scattered about under shaded pine trees give a chill to the thin air.

Finally reaching the entrance gate of Tioga Pass a new opportunity opened just for me, the eastern side of the High Sierra's. After navigating the treacherous icy downgrade through the pass, I spent the rest of the day fishing at a nice trout filled river using a glittering red spinner and camped at one of my secret spots.

On day eleven, I made camp on a ridge over looking sparkling crystal clear blue June Lake, with towering snow cover peaks in the background, just a spectacular view. I liked it so much something told me it was "heaven on earth." I went back and paid for another night.

Then I went fishing all around the June Lake Loop, using their favorite food, night crawlers. I was having the time of my life catching all kinds of big yummy, yummy cutthroat and rainbow trout surrounded by breathtaking alpine scenery. And guess what, I was even starting to look human again, with only slight sunburn on my lobster red face.

As for King George, well, the tackle shop said no one has caught him yet and the price on his head is even higher. Sure I spent hour after hour trying to catch him, but remembering what an old fisherman said about King George, I started to believe. Just like a trout fisherman, staying one foot away from hungry bears, King George was staying more than two fins away from the trout fisherman!

Waking to another beautiful sunrise on day thirteen, I started to realize the worst, of the worst, of the worst thing was happening, I was starting to run out of vacation time! However, according to the fishing treasure map, I still had enough time to camp a few nights at one of my favorite fishing spots, Lake Mary.

Lake Mary is part of the Mammoth Lakes group, which includes Lake George south of the June Lake Loop.

Lake Mary is not just your usual High Sierra Lake, what sets it apart from the other lakes in the area is of course the trout fishing. Big trout, medium trout, small trout, I don't think I have ever seen anyone who fishes in Lake Mary not catch a trout. I have seen people of all ages, kids, mom's, dads, grandmas, grandpas, big groups, small groups, and they all catch trout on any type of bait. Lake Mary must hold the record for the hungriest trout in the whole world. Who knows what the fish are eating during those winter months when the lake is completely frozen over. Whatever it is, it makes the fish hungry for anything.

The only other time I have seen fish that hungry is when I was backpacking up in Rocky Mountain National Park in Colorado, and the brook trout would hit on a plain golden hook!

Lake Mary is also known for its campgrounds. Why? Because if you are lucky, a drive-in campsite might be available right next to the lake! This means the lake is your front yard right in front of you ready for fishing, swimming or just plain gazing at the picturesque beautiful lake and glacier mountain view. Now that's the life!

But I wasn't so lucky on this particular evening driving into Lake Mary on a busy weekend. All the lake shore campsites were taken. There were still many good camp sites left under the pine trees, which is better anyways if you want peace and quite. All I wanted was peace and quite from my black bear friends.

In the very, very, early morning of day fourteen, right before sunrise with fishing pole in hand, a backpack with lunch and a small lawn chair strapped to my back, I started making my way down to the lake. The only thought I had was trying to figure out how long it would take before I caught my legal limit, "One, maybe two hours?"

Looking through the campsites, I could see that most of my fellow campers were still sleeping. Although, I did see a few dedicated fishermen stirring about and that meant the lake was all mine for picking out the best fishing spot.

Walking on a trail next to the lake I watched small white capped waves stirring up the gravel on the shoreline, and the sound of a splash far out in the middle of the lake told me a big trout was having breakfast. Taking in deep breaths of pine scented mountain air, I watched my exhale turn into a white mist. Gazing upon the night sky breaking into dawn, I thought to myself, it's at times like these, so peaceful, I would not want to be any where else in the world.

After a short stroll, I spotted a small sandy beach ahead, with just enough tree shadows for a little shade for the oncoming afternoon sun. A perfect spot, far away from the noisy campground, and a perfect spot for fishing, because of the deep pools of water created by the large granite boulders. Even the thick pine tree roots, growing into the water, created a good place to tie my fish onto keeping them cool and out of the sun.

Casting out my line using a big fat night crawler, I sat back relaxing in my lawn chair enjoying the perfect view, the kind of view you see in all those travel magazines. My eye lids felt like two ton weights were hung on them, I was so tired, I was tempted to just lie down and take a nap, but, I was also hungry for trout, and trout fishing is serious business.

And lookie, a little nibble, not a nibble, a bite! I jump up quickly, pulling the pole back hooking the fish and watch it jump out of the water into the air flipping itself around. What a fighter, a big one had my rod twitching and bending like it was ready to snap! I pulled back again holding tight, turning the reel bringing the big fish all the way in to shore.

Now for the hard part, I held the twitching pole with my left hand, knelt down on one knee grabbing my net off the ground with my other hand. I quickly stretched out my arm, pulling the tip of the pole back just enough to get the big squirming fish into the net. It was eighteen inch glowing rainbow trout!

I have a strict rule with regard to what size fish I decide to keep, must be at least twelve inches long, or even longer if the fishing regulations say different, and sometimes I don't keep any, just catch and release.

After the fish was on my stringer, I lowered him into the icy cool lake water and tied the string around a tree root. Then I started talking to the fish as if he were listening to me, "I am a trout fisherman and you are a trout, which makes you breakfast, lunch, or dinner, just like you are a fish, and eat flies, mosquitoes and worms for breakfast, lunch, or dinner. And one day I might be breakfast, lunch or dinner for the big wild bear. It's the vicious circle of life."

Re-baiting my hook with a squirming worm, excited about maybe catching my limit in record time, gave me renewed vigor. The thought of taking a nap vanished. Casting out again I notice a few small sticks floating in the water, fish sticks, ah…, my daughter and her fish sticks. What kid doesn't love fish sticks? I wish she was here right now to catch a few.

The warm sun was just starting to crest above the tree tops, sending streams of light rays through all the trees in the forest, Lake Mary, what a great place to sit back and relax enjoying the view while fishing a little. The lakes cobalt blue water sparkles with a burst of glittering silver diamonds just like a thousand little dancers of white light jumping around in every direction. The lake reflects a flawless mirror of tall pine trees, towering rugged pinnacle snow peaks surrounded by long feather clouds in a blue sky background. I didn't have a care in the world, sat back, closed my eyes, and fell into a deep, deep sleep.

I was worlds away, probably snoring, oblivious to time, or anything that might have been going on around me. Just starting to awake, slowly opening my eyes expecting to see a beautiful lake view, only the view was not of the lake, it was a big hairy, I mean really big and hairy, poop matted smelly black butt, with a stubby tail attached sticking right in my face not two feet away! I was completely trapped in the chair, blocked from even getting up by a hairy butt monster! I stared right into the butt crack of a very large hairy creature, trying to figure out what I should do. Moving my head leaning to one side, trying to see around its large mass, I watched the other end with the big nose and mouth as his paw to pull my stringer of fish towards him. In one swoop, the animal had hooked the fish with a pointed nail and brought the big squirming fish to its chomping mouth. In a big upward gulp, the three hundred plus pound black bear devoured the wiggling fish leaving a dangling stringer hanging from his lips.

I was startled. I really didn't know what to do. I couldn't fight for my fish that was no longer there, and I was literally trapped in my lawn chair by this big hairy creature's smelly butt. How could I move? Of course, I could slap the bear on his hairy butt with my hand, or give him a swift kick. However, that would make him mad, probably turning him around and likely giving me a slap back with his sharp claws and a nice bite to go with it. I really did not feel like being his main course after the trout appetizer.

The only thing I could hope for was that this bear was just like the bear who wanted to sniff trout fisherman and not eat him, not like the man eating bear I encountered in the camper shell!

Trying to ignore the smell, I made a mental note to next time move the chair further away from lake's edge putting more space between a bear butt and my butt, just in case I end up in a situation like this one again. That is, if I was going to have a next time. I also made another mental note, when in bear country don't forget to take the air horn and pepper spray wherever I go. Leaving them in the truck does not help my present situation at all.

What was the winning equation? A big butted wild black bear, + one nicely lobster face cooked trout fisherman trapped in a lawn chair, = Make a fast break before the bear takes a bite!

Now who could ask for a better view of the backside of a bear, many a scientist would probably love to take a few samples of the thick matted brown crispy doo, doo, leftovers, and look at all the stuff crawling around under a microscope.

My daughter would probably find the short stubby tail rather cute. As for me, I really hoped this bear wasn't going to fart, or decide to have a poop right in my lap!

Now what? The bear was slowly moving his big butt away from my face and bringing his head with its sharp teeth around looking me straight in the eye. I was beyond scared! He now had me completely blocked in with his huge hairy head and big fang teeth drooling bear slobber in my lap! This was not even a fight or flight situation!

I just gave up, if he was going to eat me, this was now his big chance, I could do absolutely nothing. I cringe just waiting for him to take a big bite!

Then I notice something, I could swear he was smiling! The bear just finished eating a freshly caught eighteen inch rainbow trout! I would be happy too!

So I started talking to him in a very calm voice, "Hey bear how did like that fish I caught, tasty? I bet it was tasty, but you know, if you would have let me cook it first with a little butter, lemon, and dill, over the bar-bee, it would have been a whole lot tastier. And of course you could have shared!"

Moving his big hairy head up and down, and side to side, I follow his little black eye balls looking at the bottom of my fishing pole and to what sat next to it, "Ah, you found what you were looking for, of course, my small backpack, hey it's yours but a little thank you might be in order."

Just like a happy puppy, Mr. Bear curled his paw swatting the backpack out from underneath the chair onto the small sandy beach. With one paw he held it down, and with the other he proceeded to rip the material apart spilling out all of my tasty treats. A big red apple, two granola bars, one can of root beer, and one trout sandwich loaded with Dijon mustard, lettuce, tomato, Swiss cheese and a dash of dill.

Now I could have escaped at that moment because the bear was distracted by my lunch, but I didn't, for some reason I thought we were getting along pretty good, not scared one bit.

"Hey bear, how you do like that special trout sandwich, bet you don't get to eat something like that everyday? Well you know, I'm getting hungry too and you could have some manners and give me half? But I understand, bears are wild animals surviving off what ever they can get from the land. And you are on a special diet. You are not supposed to be eating any human food at all! It's bad for you and will drive you and us humans crazy. Oh, by the way, do me a favor and please do not eat the trout fishermen."

The bear had finished eating all my lunch, took another look at me while moving his head back and forth, as if to say, "You shouldn't be feeding the bears," and, "don't you have anymore?"

Moving my head back and forth, "I didn't feed you; you stole my lunch, my snack and my rainbow trout!"

I guess the bear didn't like me accusing him of stealing, and started slowly moving towards me on his big claw paws, stuck his big head right in my lap, inches from my face sniffing with his big drooling snout. He even opened his mouth just enough to show off his big fang canine teeth, I was gagging on his terrible breath.

The time had come to say goodbye to my wife, daughter, and all my friends and family, I had my chance to run and didn't take it, looks like the big bear is finally going to eat the trout fisherman.

The bear took a twitching sniff from his wiggling black wet nose, sniffed again and again. I guess to see if I was hiding a candy bar or something in my pockets and with a little smile, a perky jump in his step, he casually walks around me scampering right back into the woods.

I couldn't believe the bear didn't eat me! I was just flabbergasted that I have another day to live! One minute I thought it was going to be all over by getting eaten by a bear, and the next minute, it's if the bear didn't come at all, I just woke up from some frightful nightmare, "Wow was I lucky!"

Looking over at what was left of my torn up backpack, I saw the reminisce of what two bear claws could do in a very short time, realizing once again how lucky I was. Now I was sure hoping that would be the end of the excitement with my wild bear friends for the day. Trying to get up to move my scared stiff body out of that chair, took more than a little effort, it was as if now that chair had become a part of me. And the bear slobber all over the front of my clothes, "Yuck!"

After re-baiting my hook again with a squirming worm, throwing out my line, I decided that if I caught another trout, I'd would go straight to the camp and cook it for lunch. Leaning my pole down on the back of my lawn chair, I walked over to the shredded back pack not seeing one morsel or crumb of food on the ground, pick up the pieces wrapping them into a clump, wondering if the bear new all along he wasn't going to eat me.

Just when I was sitting back down on my lawn chair to enjoy the view, with all the peace and quite, relaxing after surviving such a life ending experience, another fisherman comes along filled to the hilt with gear.

"Hey partner, mind if I fish here? Looks like a good spot. Been here long? Any bites? What kind of bait are you using? Hey where you from? What do you do for a living? Hey, you don't' look so good, all red, been in the sun to long, you need to use sunscreen, cancer you know, you could really use some chap stick on those lips, hey I brought a radio what do like to listen to?"

He went on and on, and on, and on. For some reason, this always happens to some trout fishermen. You have three-quarters of the lake to fish in, and some lonely fisherman sits down right next to you gabbing away! That was it for me. Explaining to the fisherman that I had a few things I needed to do back at camp, wishing him good luck, and to keep an eye out for bears.

"Bears you say? I'm not afraid of any stinking bears!"

For the rest of the day, I took long naps, explored the hiking trails, and made a trout stew with a trout from June Lake. I used a few potatoes, small can of tomato paste, onions, garlic, tarragon, basil, a bay leaf, barley, lentils, a can of green beans and other stuff.

After filling up on the fish stew, and an hour before sunset, I decided to take an evening stroll along the road that went around the lake. Fisherman were sporadically placed, some hidden behind pine trees and others were out in the open on sandy beaches. I was half way around the lake when I stopped to watch one fishermen reel in a nice big three pound fish, when out from the woods comes my smiling bear friend with his buddy. They were having a running race right for the fisherman's catch. When the fisherman heard all the crashing through the forest behind him, he turned to see the two black bears coming at full charge. Scared out of his wits yelling, "ahaaaa…," he dropped his fishing pole and took off running as fast as he could.

I started laughing so hard, I just about fell over. It was the funniest thing I had ever seen. The look on that fisherman's face! It was as if he had never seen a bear before and didn't have a clue on what to do. Of course, I am one to talk.

If they only knew what it was like, to have a wild bear chasing after you going around, and around a truck. Or, a growling big bear two inches from your face, while you're stuffed in a sleeping bag. Or, to be trapped in a lawn chair, by the dirty butt of a black bear you didn't know if it was going to poop on you, or eat you, now that is scary! But come on, you don't need to leave a perfectly good fishing pole behind, because a few hungry bears want some easy picking trout!

After the bears were done gobbling up the fisherman's trout, a task which took of about two minutes, they started sniffing the ground following the thick wooded shore line.

I followed right behind as they came upon another fisherman repeating the previous scenario. The bears had absolutely no fear of humans, and why should they? Unsuspecting fisherman on seeing the bears scream to the top of their lungs in fear, dropping fishing poles, running away as fast as they can, leaving behind freshly caught rainbow trout and small back packs full of goodies.

These two bears have a thought out plan with one goal in mind, to eat as many trout as a bear can eat! One might even call it a bear smorgasbord.

I have never laughed so hard in my whole life, watching those bears pick off one unsuspecting fisherman, after fisherman, as they made their way halfway around the lake before they were full. It was such good entertainment. Did I feel sorry for the trout fisherman? Sure, but trout fisherman should always remember, Mr. Wild Bear could come at any time to steal the yummy trout. Thank goodness the Lake Mary bears have only decided to eat the trout, and not the trout fisherman, so far.

I would not be surprised at all, if when the time does come and all the trout have almost disappeared from overfishing a sign will be posted at every lake, river and stream saying, "Don't feed the wild bears! (Especially trout fisherman!)" Because the bears will want the next best thing to a trout, a trout fisherman! Every camper will be pointing at me and other trout fisherman telling the hungry bear, "Don't eat me! Eat him, he's the trout fisherman!"

The following fifteenth day in late afternoon, I was coming down from the trail finishing up on a three hour hike ending at the trail head parking lot. I noticed three bears sniffing around a small car, "Uh oh, this does not look good."

The biggest one of the black bears, which was almost the size of the small car himself, got up on his hind legs and put his two big paws on the passenger side window of a mid size car. With no resistance the glass shattered into a million pieces. Wasting no time the big bear somehow squeezed half of his body into the window opening sniffing around before he found the prize and pulled himself back out. Moving his big head back and forth, he showed his bear buddies the prized possession, the wrapper of a snicker's bar. His bear friends gathered around him to take a sniff of the prized treat, before heading to other cars in the parking lot.

When these people come back to their car, after having a fun little hike, they will find a new window has been open for air conditioning. At first they probably will think vandals got into the car. Looking further, seeing nothing was stolen, and noticing the big bear print on the ripped seat, they will realize it was a bear.

Some people don't think they need to read all the bear warning signs at the trail heads, only later to find out the hard way with a new improved air condition window soon be sealed over with plastic wrap and duck tape. And yet these people don't know how really lucky they were, to only have a new improved air conditioning window to worry about, and not a whole door missing.

One time, at Crater Lake in Oregon, I remember witnessing the aftermath of a Volkswagen bug having its whole door ripped off by a hungry bear that was going after an ice chest inside. The owner was not impressed by the improvements at all!

With my fishing trip now coming to an end, I felt very lucky to now have a few stubbles on the top of my head popping up, my singed off eyebrows were starting to grow back and the orange glow on my face was looking more like bad sunburn. I will never be able to wash my clothes enough times to get all the bear slobber off, my ripped sleeping bag and backpack are going to have to be replaced, or saved as souvenirs. A nice memento reminder from the wildlife partying I had with my bear friend to go along with the picture I took of him.

When I tell everyone back home about my trout fishing vacation, some people will think I was very unlucky because of all the life threatening encounters with the bears and the fire pit explosion experience. But I think I had a great trout fishing vacation because of all the yummy fresh trout I was able to catch, (thanks to my trout fishing treasure map), the breathtaking scenery I was able to enjoy, and the peace and quite of camping in the great outdoors.

But, best of all, despite all of my bear encounters on this trout fishing trip, and over the years, none of the bears have been lucky enough to actually succeed in eating the trout fisherman, i.e. me.

The End

Bear Facts

Brown bears are the Alaskan, Grizzly, European, Syrian and Kodiak. Males weigh between 400 to 1200 pounds, with females weighing 300 to 800 pounds. Their diet consist of plants, insects, beetles, termites, worms, fish, and will hunt for prey, such as rodents, small animals, even deer. Brown bears have been known to migrate long distances, even a couple hundred miles, in search of food.

The life span of a brown bear in the wild is around twenty-five years. During that time, a female can give birth to one or two baby bears each year.

Brown bears hibernate, between October to March, in dens to conserve energy during the long winter because less food in available. They can be awaken easily at anytime, if disturbed.

Black bears are found only in North America and come in different colors, blue-gray, cinnamon, white and of course black. Male bears weight between 125 pounds to more than 600 pounds, and females from 90 pounds to over 300 pounds eating mostly fruits, nuts, grasses and insect larvae.

The life of a span of a black bear in the wild is eighteen to twenty-five years and females usually have two or three cubs each year.

Black bears are good swimmers, tree climbers and can run thirty-five miles an hour. They hibernate, and can go without food for seven months.

Asian Black Bears are recognized by a white crescent shape on the chest area. These bears live only in Asia deep in the mountain terrain and prefer being in trees than on the ground.

They weight between 225 to 400 pounds eating fruits, nuts, termites, sheep and even small cows. Asian black bears can hibernate, but only if they want to.

Sloth Bear is so named because it looks like a Sloth. The bears can weight form 250-300 pounds living off fruits but mostly ants and termites sucking then up into their mouths without teeth. These bears do not hibernate and can be found throughout Asia, mostly in Sri Lanka and India.

Spectacled Bear has rings of color around the eyes, white or golden, with a dark brown or black fur body. They live only in warm areas of South America and can range form 175 to 400 pounds living mostly of plants, but will eat meat. These bears do not hibernate.

Sun Bear is usually less than 100 pounds, making it the smallest bear in the world. They have dark fur, and prefer sitting in the sun all day in the warm climates of Cambodia, Malaysia, Bangladesh, Burma, Vietnam and Borneo. Like most bears, they eat fruits, nuts and will eat rodents but, what this bear loves to eat more than anything else is, honey. The Sun bear does not hibernate.

Panda Bears are very unique because of the mostly white fur covering the body except for the black rings around the eyes, front and back legs, and a black streak that goes over the shoulders. Panda Bears live in the thick damp forest of China, weighing up to two hundred pounds, eating bamboo shoots in areas that are plentiful. They also eat other plants and small animals.

Polar Bears have adapted well to the frozen artic environment, hunting mostly seals in the cold water. Polar Bears have completely white fur, can weigh up to 1700 pounds, run twenty-five miles and hour and swim sixty miles without resting. Polar Bears are found in Alaska, Canada, Norway, Russia and Greenland. Females build dens to have their young, giving birth to twin cubs. The male continues to roam, taking no part in raising the cubs and may even kill them.

Koala Bear is not really a bear; early Australia settlers thought it was a bear because of the way it looked. The Koala is related to marsupial mammals that have pouches to carry their babies such as wallabies, possums, wombats, kangaroos etc.

Teddy Bear, a stuff bear was made and named "Teddy" in response to a bear hunting fiasco incident in 1902 down in Mississippi in which U.S. President Theodore Roosevelt, whose nick name was "Teddy," was involved. The political hot potato did not survive long, but the Teddy Bear did selling hundreds even today.

ABOUT THE AUTHOR

Over the past many years, writing stories have become a serious passion of mine, relying on the memories of growing up with five brothers, four sisters and reliving the memories of an outdoors-man who has traveled the world seeking the evasive trout.

Working as a Building Inspector / General Contractor, I have resided in California, Oregon, Washington, Hawaii, Sweden, and have always carried a sense of humor with me, along with my fishing pole.

Danny McGee currently lives in Northern California, in the small town of Windsor with his wife and daughter, surrounded by trout rivers, trout lakes, giant redwood trees and still occasionally runs into and away from, his friend the hungry bear.

Note:

Danny McGee the trout fisherman is not to be confused with other Danny McGee's that might be running around.

Other Books written by -
                Danny McGee

****

The Biggest Spider in the Whole World in Mrs. Higgins Kitchen Sink!

****

Sleeping With a Zillion Big Spiders and A Few Rattle Snakes!

****

GREENHORN!

****

Wave Head

****

Don't feed the wild bears! (Especially trout fisherman!)